A WEAVER'S LIFE

ETHEL MAIRET

1872 ✿ 1952

MARGOT COATTS

*crafts*council

in association with the Crafts Study Centre, Bath

© Crafts Study Centre, Bath 1983

ISBN 0 903798 70 0

Published by the Crafts Council
12 Waterloo Place
London SW1Y 4AU

Designed by Philip Miles

Printed in Great Britain
by Jolly & Barber Ltd
Rugby, Warwickshire

Photographic credits

Colour photography by David Cripps

Black-and-white photography: Gerd Bergerson, 90; David Cripps, 35, 87 (top); James Phillips, 87 (bottom); Guy Ryecart 1, 25, 27, 49, 50, 51, 52, 100, 101; Marianne Straub, 91; Colin Wilson, 53

Photographs of historical documents by Colin Wilson and James Phillips, University of Bath

The cover illustration is a detail from a scarf in vegetable-dyed eri silk warp and vegetable-dyed pashmina weft (pashmina is the under-fur of the cashmere goat); plain weave with crammed weft stripes in cream and brown pashmina: Gospels Workshop, c. 1930. Victoria and Albert Museum. Photograph by Ian Dobbie.

The photograph at the front of the book shows the oak signboard for Ethel Mairet's workshop at Gospels, designed and cut by Eric Gill

CONTENTS

ACKNOWLEDGEMENTS

The Ethel Mairet Research Project was initiated in 1981 by the Crafts Study Centre at the Holburne of Menstrie Museum, University of Bath, and was made possible by generous grants from the Crafts Council and the Worshipful Company of Weavers. Travel to the United States for research was kindly funded by the British Academy. I have also benefited from being an associate member of the Centre for the History of Technology, Science and Society at the University of Bath.

Special thanks for support and assistance are due to my colleagues and advisers: the Trustees of the Crafts Study Centre, in particular Professor Christopher Frayling and Marianne Straub, Barley Roscoe (Crafts Study Centre), Marigold Coleman (Crafts Council) and John Styles (University of Bath).

I am indebted to Alan Crawford, Dr Roger Lipsey and Dr Durai Raja Singam for leading me to information on the Ceylon and Campden periods of Ethel Mairet's life, and to Felicity Ashbee and Dr Rama Coomaraswamy for permission to reproduce family material in this context. For permission to quote from his writings and for giving additional information on Philip Mairet's life, I am grateful to Charles Sisson, Violet Welton and Philip Mairet's executors. For background information on the Saunton period, I thank Iona Smyth Reed, and for the Ditchling period thanks are due to Mary Hill, Stopford Jacks, Margery Kendon, Janet Leach, Joan Partridge and Petra Tegetmeier who, with many others from the Mairet circle and Gospels workshop, have patiently helped to piece the story together. Ethel Mairet's exhibitions have been elucidated by Dorothy Hutton and Muriel

Rose and assistance has also been given by the Red Rose Guild.

Museums which I have consulted are Birmingham Museum and Art Gallery, the Gallery of English Costume at Platt Hall, Manchester, the Museum of London and the Victoria and Albert Museum (Departments of Metalwork and Textiles, Indian Section). I have researched material at several libraries: Bath University; Bath Reference Library; Camberwell School of Art and Crafts; the Museum of Fine Arts in Boston; the CoSIRA Library in Salisbury; the Fawcett Society Library, City of London Polytechnic; the Visual Collections, Fogg Art Museum, Harvard University; the Modern Literary Archive at King's College, Cambridge; the Firestone Library at Princeton University; the Royal Academy of Music; and the National Art Library at the Victoria and Albert Museum.

I should like to thank the authors (or their executors) and the publishers for quoted material, and also all those who have lent or given documents or textiles to the Crafts Study Centre during the course of research. Among the latter are Mary Barker, Marion Boniface, Ray Leigh of the Campden Trust, Elizabeth Clifford, Peter Collingwood, Kate Crofton, Esmé Davis, Joyce Griffiths, the Guild of St Joseph and St Dominic, Fay Hankins, Ellen Mayne, Joy Sinden, Edith Solomon, Marianne Straub and Robert Welch. Alistair and Rosemary Voaden and family have patiently allowed their house to be photographed, as have Stuart Jolly, Tom Mcarthur, John Piper, Roger Redfarn and Marc Urquhart. Gwen and Barbara Mullins have assisted by housing certain textiles for the Crafts Study Centre, and Brandon Cadbury has aided us financially in the conservation of drawings.

Unique and valuable criticism has been offered by John Houston, to whom I am deeply grateful, and also to Hilary Chetwynd who taught me the rudiments of weaving.

Finally I should like to thank my willing collaborators, the photographers who have contributed so greatly to this book – David Cripps, Guy Ryecart, James Phillips and Colin Wilson – and the editor, Judy Walker.

Margot Coatts
March 1983

FOREWORD

Historical research into the origins and development of twentieth-century British crafts – the people, their connections, their philosophies, their workshops, the cultural significance of their work – has for a long time lagged behind research into the equivalent history of modern design for mass-production. There have, of course, been many attempts to trace the development of a particular medium or material used by craftspeople, and even more attempts to compile illustrated books about "how to do it", but on the whole the complex traditions out of which contemporary craft work has emerged have been seriously neglected by scholars and critics alike. *Pioneers of Modern Craft* is a book that remains to be written.

There are many reasons for this. Where the actual research is concerned, there is the problem of tracking down the written evidence (in the form of recipe books, accounts, diaries, letters, reminiscences) out of which such a history could be constructed: a rather special problem where most crafts-people are concerned. Where the framework of the study is concerned, William Morris and C. R. Ashbee have usually been treated in the literature as pioneers of modern *design*, part of a dominant tradition which led from the Arts and Crafts Movement, via the Bauhaus, to the final design solutions of the 1920s and 1930s: the influence of Morris and Ashbee on the history of British craftsmanship in this century – at all levels – has tended to be implied rather than explored in detail. Where the historical philosophy of the study is concerned, there are the published statements of well-known craftspeople who were never sure (or did not care) whether they belonged to the history of art (in which case the art historians could tell their story) or to the history of design (in which case architectural historians could do the same). Above all, there is the complexity of today's craft scene, where the work of makers from the three main traditions of craft activity in the twentieth century – the Arts and Crafts tradition, the Council of Industrial Design tradition and, most recently, the "craftsman's art" tradition – all goes under the general (if occasionally misleading) title of "the crafts": some of these makers are highly mindful of the traditions to which they belong, others are slightly embarrassed about them, and others try to cut themselves off entirely.

The rôle of the Crafts Study Centre in Bath is to encourage studies of the life and work of British artist-craftspeople in the twentieth century, and – through the Centre's rapidly expanding archive, collection, exhibition programme and library – to make available as wide a variety of materials as possible for such studies, so that makers, critics, researchers and enthusiasts can look for (and at) the roots of contemporary work in the crafts. This book, and the exhibition which accompanies it, grew out of a Crafts Study Centre research project, and in the future the Centre aims to launch a major project of this calibre every two years. The hope is that the resulting body of work will eventually provide the materials for a major re-assessment of the origins and development of modern British crafts. At that stage, it may even be possible for *Pioneers of Modern Craft* to be written.

In what ways was Ethel Mairet a "pioneer"? Today we take for granted so many of the ideas she originated that it is very difficult to judge the extent of her contribution. Hamada once called Ethel Mairet "the mother of English hand-weaving", and Margot Coatts's researches have confirmed that through Ethel Mairet's writings, her workshops, her apprentices and her contacts with India, Yugoslavia and Scandinavia, she helped to found (or, as she might have preferred it, to re-discover) the tradition of modern hand-weaving in England – a tradition which laid special emphasis on texture and yarn as opposed to pattern. During all the various phases of her professional life, from the early Arts and Crafts years to the latter years at Gospels when she was a source of inspiration to several designers in the textile industry, this appears to have been the consistent theme: "You got your inspiration from the loom . . . You did what the spirit moved you to do." In less sensitive hands (and there were plenty of those around in the middle years of this century) Ethel Mairet's approach to hand-weaving could easily have become rather precious and "arty-crafty" – a lame justification for the use of poor-quality "rustic" yarns and an amateur attitude towards designing – but she succeeded in avoiding this by a life-time's study of yarns and yarn types, and by an intuitive appreciation of colour. Many of her apprentices and associates have recalled that Ethel Mairet's greatest gift to them was colour, the work they did in the dye-shed at Gospels. C. R. Ashbee's assessment appears to have been a just one: "She has the soul of Oriental colour in her."

A Weaver's Life tells the story of Ethel Mairet as self-taught weaver, spinner and dyer. Largely through reminiscences by her colleagues and students, the book also traces her influence as teacher, writer, collector and entrepreneur. The picture of Ethel Mairet that emerges from the story is one of a fiercely independent, strong-willed designer who was not always the easiest person to work with, but who managed to communicate her enthusiasms to everyone she taught. Ethel Mairet did not care very much about what other people thought of her and she was never as strong on techniques as she was on yarn and colour – "an intelligence rather of feeling than of brain". But the most long-lasting impression of Ethel Mairet that emerges from *A Weaver's Life* is of an inspiring teacher, a catalyst during a crucial period in the development of British crafts: as she wrote, "Most artist-craftsmen have served no real apprenticeship, but have come to the study of their craft by the study of art. We owe more to travel, museums, private study and technical books than to intimacy with past masters of our work; and most craftsmen are now agreed that this is a disadvantage. We need this living, oral and practical continuity of education. Our workshops must become schools of workmanship, producing good workers as well as good work . . . We must not merely praise the old training by apprenticeship, but take and teach apprentices."

This was certainly true of Ethel Mairet, and it is still true today.

Christopher Frayling
Professor and Head of the Department of Cultural History,
Royal College of Art
Chairman of Trustees, Crafts Study Centre
March 1983

CHAPTER 1
FORMATIVE YEARS
1872 - 1902

The first child of Mary and James Partridge, Ethel Mary Partridge was born in 1872 in Barnstaple, on the north Devon coast. Two younger children followed: a sister Maud, born in 1874, and a brother Frederick James born in 1876. Little is known about their upbringing but it was, one suspects, modest: James Partridge was a dispensing chemist in Pilton, near Barnstaple, and Fred attended Barnstaple Grammar School. The family were Non-Conformists and members of the Congregational Church but Ethel Mary, as she was called, followed no religion for most of her adult life.

Ethel Mary and Fred Partridge soon showed artistic leanings. The fragmentary evidence shows that Ethel Mary received a prize at Barnstaple School of Art in 1891 and Fred attended the Birmingham Municipal School of Art between 1899 and 1901. Here he doubtless obtained his silversmithing skills, and he subsequently returned to attend classes at Barnstaple.

In the late nineteenth-century several Arts and Crafts figures were working in and around the town. W. R. Lethaby (born in Barnstaple in 1857) was articled to a local architect until 1879 when he left to join Norman Shaw's office in London. By 1896 he had become the Principal of the new Central School of Arts and Crafts, one of the first official bastions of the crafts revival. In 1879 the Brannam Pottery, renowned for the Barum Ware much loved by Ethel Mairet all her life, was established, and from 1816 to 1906 E. B. Fishley was running his pottery at Fremington, famous for slip-decorated earthenware. It was the practical wares of Fishley which so impressed Ethel Mairet's contemporaries Bernard Leach, Shoji Hamada and Michael Cardew when they began slipware trials at St Ives. Jack Bailey, who had worked at

C. R. Ashbee's Guild of Handicraft in East London, founded the Barnstaple Guild of Metalworkers in 1901; Fred Partridge belonged briefly to this before going on to the Guild of Handicraft in Chipping Campden (no doubt on Bailey's recommendation), where he became the first link in the chain of Ethel's direct involvement with the Ashbees and, more importantly, with the crafts ethic.

Viewed in this light, Barnstaple does not seem such a backwater for an aspiring craftsman at the turn of the century, and it seems likely that the young Ethel Partridge early espoused the principles of Morris and Ruskin.

Little is known about the years 1891–1902 in Ethel Partridge's life, except that she taught at an art school during this period, and one can only guess that this was in Barnstaple. We do know, however, that during the 1890s she studied music and was awarded a Royal Academy of Music teacher's diploma for pianoforte in 1899. With this qualification she took a post as governess, first in London and later in Bonn in Germany.

By 1902 Ethel Partridge had returned to England. Hunting fossils on the

The earliest record of Ethel Partridge's artistic leanings, awarded when she was 19; the prize was Ruskin's book The Two Paths: Lectures on Art *and* The Eagle's Nest: Lectures on the Relation of Natural Science to Art

*Ethel Coomaraswamy photographed by
Ananda Coomaraswamy after their
marriage in 1902.
By courtesy of Robert Welch
Right: Ethel (standing), Fred and Maud
Partridge, c. 1880. By courtesy of Joan Partridge*

north Devon coast she met Ananda Kentish Coomaraswamy, a brilliant Anglo-Ceylonese who had recently received a first class degree in geology and botany from the University of London, and who was shortly to leave for Ceylon to carry out an official mineralogical survey of the island. Their relationship was an instant success for they married on 19 June 1902, when Ethel was 30 and Ananda 25. The marriage would have met with some prejudice in English and Indian society, although no doubt it was thought admirable by most of the couple's artistic friends.

Another important relationship was formed at this time, with C. R. Ashbee, leader of the Guild of Handicraft, and his wife Janet. The Guild had recently moved from London to Chipping Campden in the Cotswolds and the initial contact was made by Fred Partridge who joined the Guild in the summer of 1902 as a jeweller. A further link was provided by May Hart, a talented jeweller and friend of the Ashbees, who later became Fred Partridge's wife.

The nature of the community in Campden, experimental in both artistic and social terms, inspired the Coomaraswamys to settle there and they enlisted the help of the Ashbees in finding a home for their return from Ceylon five years later.

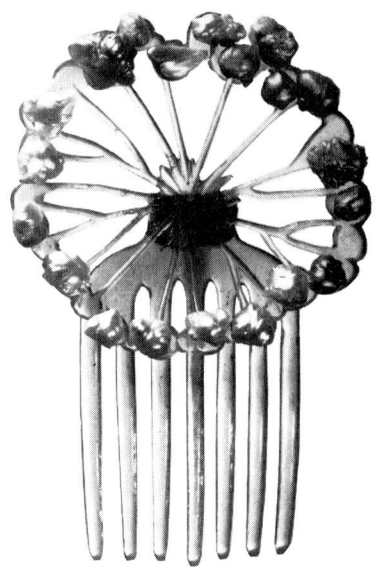

A hair comb made by Fred Partridge in 1905–10, after he left the Guild of Handicraft. The comb is made of horn, mounted with baroque pearls, and has a silver hinge. Presented by Mrs Ann Hull Grundy to Birmingham City Museum and Art Gallery

CHAPTER 2
ARTS AND CRAFTS
IN CEYLON
1903-1906

The Coomaraswamys left for Ceylon very early in 1903, taking with them all the paraphernalia for the work of the geological survey. They settled in a bungalow just outside the old capital Kandy, high in the centre of the island.*

Ceylon at the beginning of the twentieth century was based on an export economy, run by a middle class which followed the English model and system of values. Ananda Coomaraswamy found this society unacceptable, partly because it reflected the views of his father, the distinguished Ceylonese barrister Sir Mutu Coomaraswamy, who had died in 1879. From the age of two Ananda Coomaraswamy had been brought up by his mother as an Englishman and encouraged to minimise his Indian blood. Only on two previous occasions had he returned to Ceylon as an adult, both visits connected with geology. He was very aware of the results of English influence and his stay of 1903–6, although intended to be primarily scientific, found him increasingly drawn to the study of pre-colonial art and society. The influence of Ruskin and Morris, whose writings were owned and recommended to him by Ethel, was a great stimulus. Roger Lipsey wrote of his transference of interest from geology to art:

That Coomaraswamy felt drawn toward an active role in society was the natural consequence of his father's example and heredity; that he became a student of the history of art must be due, in part, to an intimate process of awakening to his

---

*Dr Roger Lipsey and Dr Durai Raja Singam have made detailed studies of Ananda Coomaraswamy's life and work, and it is to them that we owe most of the information about this period. *See the Bibliography (page 127) for details of their publications relating to Coomaraswamy.*

individuality. It will be clear in what follows that the history of art was never for him either a light question – one that had to do only with pleasures – or a question of scholarship for its own sake, but rather a question of setting right what had gone amiss partly through ignorance of the past.[1]

For Ethel Coomaraswamy life in Ceylon included accompanying her husband on his many field trips, travelling by bullock cart and on foot through splendid and difficult country (so dense that the succeeding director of the geological project was lost in the jungle in 1909). It was almost certainly due to her influence that on these expeditions they also recorded the arts and crafts of each village. They made several visits to the museum in Colombo and also sought out private collections. Ethel Coomaraswamy took numerous documentary photographs, at the same time keeping a meticulous record in her journals of each item photographed and each craft observed. The Coomaraswamys' research, begun almost as soon as they arrived in Ceylon, was published on their return to England in a large volume, *Mediaeval Sinhalese Art*, still the recognised authority on the subject. Ananda's name appears alone on the title page, but his dedication acknowledges the assistance of his wife, "my comrade in this undertaking". In a letter to the *Ceylon Observer*, addressed to the Kandyan chiefs, he expressed his feelings about the disappearance of craftsmen practising the minor arts:

During the last two years, I have given my spare time to studying old Kandyan work in architecture and all the crafts that flourished in those times that seem now so far away. I have seen old buildings and new; and in the minor arts it has not been once or twice only that I have attempted to get made for myself some one or other of the wares that were once produced so easily and so well, and of which a little of the wreckage survives in a few museums and private collections; and it has been again and again borne in upon me as the result of bitter experience both in the remotest villages and in Kandy itself, that the character of steady competence which once distinguished the Kandyan artist craftsman has gone forever; a change such as the industrial revolution has brought about almost all over the world.[2]

Not only did Coomaraswamy involve himself with the visual arts of Ceylon, he also took up the causes of literature and music; in the latter Ethel, a trained pianist, was once again his collaborator, able to offer practical knowledge to substantiate his theoretical views. He led others, mostly of European extraction, in the formation of the Ceylon Social Reform Society, active from 1905 to 1909. The Society expounded the spirit of nationalism which was currently sweeping India, resulting in the remodelling of Ceylon's Constitution in 1910. Ananda Coomaraswamy was seen as a more idealistic

Exterior and interior views of Rock Villa near Kandy in Ceylon, where the Coomaraswamys lived from 1903 to 1904. The interior view shows Ananda Coomaraswamy at work in his study. Exterior courtesy of Dr S. Durai Raja Singam; interior courtesy of Dr Rama Coomaraswamy

reformer, acting through the medium of the Society's journal, the *Ceylon National Review*, the first such journal in the country. The second issue contained his well-argued article, "Anglicisation of the East", in which he deplored the wearing of European clothes, the adoption of Western manners, art and music, and the eating of meat. He supported the teaching of Oriental history, religions and languages and assisted in founding the India Society in London in 1910–11, remaining a member of its executive committee until 1916.

At this formative stage in her career, Ethel Mairet clearly gained much inspiration from her first husband, but it would be a mistake to conclude that she lived in his shadow in any way. From the first she pursued her interests in the crafts, and in embroidery in particular, which she taught at the Clarence Memorial School in Kandy, and also to a class of Ceylonese ladies in Colombo. Ananda Coomaraswamy's appendix to his wife's embroidery section in *Mediaeval Sinhalese Art* records that her students showed excellent work in the Ceylon Society of Arts exhibitions of 1905 and 1906 and that prizes were awarded. He continues:

But the best evidence of the value of such work was the interest awakened in old traditions and designs, as, for example, in the case of the daughter of a Kandyan chief who brought to the class a highly valued memorial of the past, a jacket . . . and made a very excellent copy of the sleeve.[3]

The appendix also reports that the Inspectress of Needlework had abolished the worst abuses of needlework in Ceylonese schools where "all things Victorian" still lingered on, notably the lurid and unimaginative Berlin woolwork.

Ethel Coomaraswamy's first article on Sinhalese embroidery, published in the *Ceylon National Review* in July 1906, gives an account of how she became interested in the subject.

I was staying at Haldummulla; we had a visit from an ex-Arachchi of a neighbouring village, who brought with him some of his household treasures to show us. Among them was a large bag, made of fine blue cloth with embroidered work on it in red and white cotton. He explained this was a precious possession which no money would make him part with, and that it had been in his family for generations. This was my first experience of this kind of work and I thereupon made up my mind to get to know more about it.[4]

She discovered that "in out-of-the-way villages some old men could be found who know the stitches"[5], and these she copied. The woven cotton cloth on which the embroidery was worked was made by only one or two native Ceylonese families, although the Tamil people wove in the north and east; from her description of the weaving process it is already possible to discern a strong, if ill-informed, interest. Materials (all cotton), stitches, styles and designs are painstakingly and methodically described with the declared interest of a practitioner; she even allows European embroidery as long as it is not "the kind with patterns stamped on linen or cloth to be worked with shaded colours in silk or cotton that do not wash properly or else fade into bad colours". Already the tone of her writings is practical and more than a little dogmatic; her closing lines, however, are the often-quoted words of William Morris: "Have nothing in your houses that you do not know to be useful or believe to be beautiful."[6]

The mutual excitement engendered by their cultural and geological discoveries in Ceylon provided the Coomaraswamys with the material for many articles and papers. Ananda Coomaraswamy sent back to England a barrage of maps, reports and articles which, as part of the mineralogical survey, earned him his doctorate; he was the first Ceylonese to be awarded a DSc from London University. In addition he had discovered a new mineral, thorianite.

Together the Coomaraswamys published an essay entitled "Kandyan Horn Combs",[7] and Ethel went on to publish her own thoughts on embroidery, "Embroidery and Dress", in the English magazine *The Dress Review*.[8] In this she again quotes William Morris, and she also praises the embroidery of the Orient, referring particularly to vegetable dyes for which she claims to know "a little of the technique". Her analysis of the design failure of "three-dimensional" Chinese embroidery is most interesting and serves to reinforce her view of the desirability of a flat-patterned surface.

The Dress Review itself should not pass without mention; it was promoted by the Healthy and Artistic Dress Union, which included the Arts and Crafts movement on its committee in the shape of people like Janet Ashbee and Godfrey Blount. The Union had been founded in 1890 for "the propagation of sound ideas on the subject of dress" and the first articles were on subjects such as "Corset Wearing: the Medical Side of the Attack" and "Progress in Taste and Dress in Relation to Art Education". The illustrations showed loose, simple garments, befitting the new sports of tennis and cycling. The early dress reformists were also interested in "art embroidered" fabrics and Eastern draperies, mostly obtained from Liberty's. As well as her article on embroidery, Ethel Mairet published two articles on dress reform in *The Dress Review*: her translation of "The Dress Movement in Germany"[9] (April 1903) and "English Dress in the Colonies"[10] (October 1905). Ananda Coomaraswamy and Janet Ashbee also contributed articles during the same period.

Ethel Coomaraswamy wrote several further articles on Ceylon, including one on the "Education of Girls in Ceylon"[11] and "Music in Ceylon".[12] In both articles she advocates a sound study of Ceylonese culture and history; in music she recommends the *vina* or *tamburi* (rather like a long-necked guitar) above the piano, and in art the keeping of the Indian tradition of drawing and pattern design: "Nothing could be more calculated to stamp out all individuality than the methods of South Kensington."[13] (A reference to the Department of Science and Art, whose operations were constantly criticised by members of the Arts and Crafts Movement.)

The Coomaraswamys stayed in Kandy for slightly less than a year before moving down to Colombo where they took a large residence called Ishabella Court in Galle Road. With reference to this period of her life, she later wrote to Ashbee: "It is rather nice to fare sumptuously every day – for a time – we had spells of it in Ceylon. But it palls horribly in the long run."[14]

During the five years in Ceylon plans had been progressing for the conversion of the Norman Chapel at Broad Campden into a house for the Coomaras (as they were frequently called) to live in when they returned; in 1903 Ashbee had surveyed the building and, being unable to afford to convert it from dereliction himself, had recommended it to Ananda, probably during the second half of 1905. By 1906 plans for the conversion were being exchanged, with Ethel Coomaraswamy adding cryptic comments to the design. Of the nave, which was to be used as the music room, she noted to Ashbee: "This must be our sitting room and music room. Accordingly it *must* have a fireplace, I cannot *stand* a stove."[15] (In the event, Ethel's bourgeois leanings were squashed for, although a fireplace was added, the room was used not as a music room but as the site of the Essex House Press.) The restoration of the chapel absorbed the services of the Guild of Handicraft for over a year and even a stonemason's yard was set up on the site. All this was made possible by Ananda's inheritance of "a very considerable fortune".[16]

During the second half of the nineteenth century and the first decade of the twentieth century, Britain was gripped with a craze for embroidery. At Camberwell School of Art and Crafts, for example, embroidery and dress design were on the 1907 syllabus while weaving was not.[17] Without doubt, Ethel Coomaraswamy's interest in the textile arts sprang from studying pre-colonial Kandyan embroideries (before 1815) which were brought to her or found in museums. From these examples she adapted her own technique from the European to the Sinhalese tradition, at least for the purposes of teaching. At the Norman Chapel she embroidered regularly and also in Ceylon.

At the same time, Ethel Coomaraswamy had become curious about the

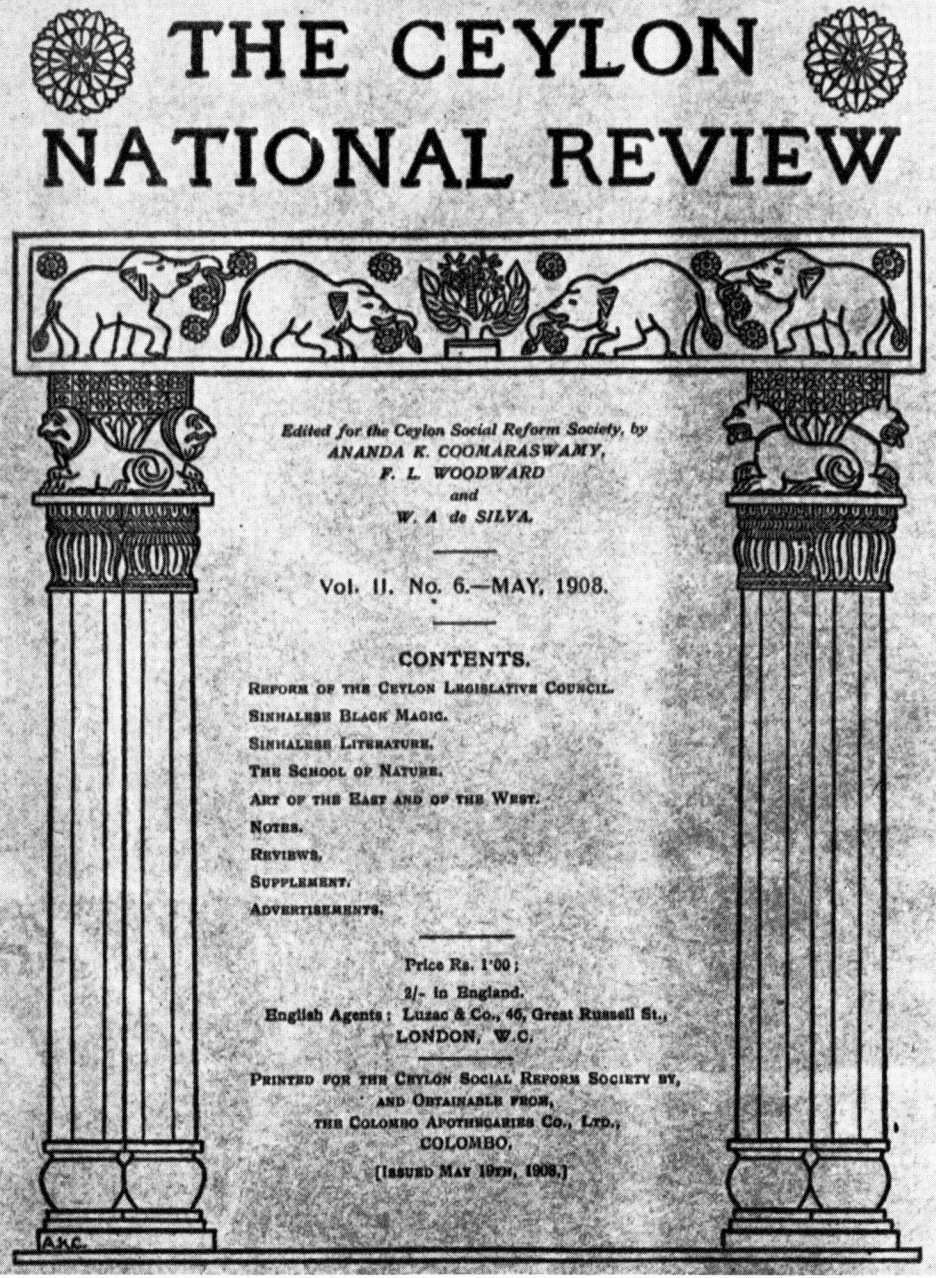

The title page of the Ceylon National Review, *the journal of the Ceylon Social Reform Society. By courtesy of Dr S. Durai Raja Singam*

Ethel Coomaraswamy took many documentary photographs of the arts and crafts of Ceylon, later used to illustrate Mediaeval Sinhalese Art *by Ananda K. Coomaraswamy. The illustration opposite, showing the recurrent motif of birds with intertwined necks, is from the metalwork chapter*

cloth on which Kandyan embroidery was worked. For *Mediaeval Sinhalese Art* she had photographed raw cotton being prepared in a mangle or cotton gin, spindle spun and then woven. The full length of the warp was stretched on the ground while the weaver sat with feet in a pit. Passages in *Mediaeval Sinhalese Art* describe plain weave, then continue with a detailed description of patterned cloth, showing that the processes had been minutely observed:

To make geometrical patterns, the necessary warp threads are picked up with a narrow lath or weaver's sword (*sema lella*), and a wider lath is then inserted and turned up sideways so as to form a "shed" for the passage of the shuttle. Before the sword is pulled out again, slips of cane are passed between the separated warp threads behind the heddles; there they accumulate and preserve the pattern, making it easy to pick up the threads again when the pattern is repeated or reversed.

There is a tradition to the effect that in the time of the mythical King Maha Sammata, in the course of a great war, all looms were destroyed by fire; and the form of the heddles was only preserved in the ashes, which lay undisturbed in the form of them; and hence the name *aluva*, from *alu*, ashes, instead of the former name *umandave*. This popular etymology is quite fanciful.[18]

A description of irregular patterns being put in by a tapestry or inlay technique follows, and in her journals she records that on one occasion a native family came to weave in her compound. The vegetable dyeing of yarns with madder and indigo had almost disappeared and is referred to only in passing, but the preparation and dyeing of niyanda leaf fibre, used for weaving mats, is fully explained, and the book describes how the plant *patangi* had to be boiled for three days and nights to obtain the finest and most permanent of reds. It seems that although Ethel Coomaraswamy learnt the rudiments of weaving in Ceylon, she learnt little about the art of dyeing to which she was later to devote herself.[19] Her sensitivity to colour, however, was already apparent in her articles on embroidery.

On 28 December 1906 Ananda Coomaraswamy completed his appointment as director of the mineralogical survey, and they left Ceylon for a three-month tour of India. While in Ceylon, Ethel had suffered a miscarriage, the first of what Janet Ashbee called "her tragedies";[20] she was never to have any children of her own.

In India, as in Ceylon, the Coomaras collected a wealth of *objets d'art* and paintings, at the same time adding to their appreciation of these by studying India's languages, religious traditions and cultural heritage. The fine collection which was assembled on this and later occasions was offered later to the Government of India for a museum in Benares, but it was not accepted, the importance of the artefacts not yet being acknowledged. After he and Ethel separated, Coomaraswamy took the nucleus of his collection with him to America in 1917, and much of it eventually found a home in the Museum of Fine Arts, Boston, where he had been appointed Curator of Indian Art.

CHAPTER 3
THE NORMAN CHAPEL
1907 - 1910

When the Coomaraswamys returned to England in 1907, they moved into the Norman Chapel. The renovation of the building had excited much interest in Campden, and in the broader context of the contemporary architectural press. *The Builder* published an account of "the repair and restoration of the old building, the building of a new wing, and the laying out of a formal garden."[1] An even more lengthy article, written by C. R. Ashbee and illustrated by his draughtsman Philip Mairet, appeared in *The Studio* of the same year.[2] Printed here is a recent assessment of the scheme by the architectural historian Alan Crawford:

It was proposed at first that the nave should be used as a music room, and the awkward fact that its late mediaeval ceiling had been laid so destructively low that it broke across the top of the Norman chancel arch was got round by raising the easternmost ceiling bay. This change of level became, in the Library above, a dais at one end, which, curtained off with rich Morris fabrics, provided a marvellous inner sanctum for the Sinhalese scholar. As for the rest of the building, Ashbee handled it with all the tact one would expect of an architect who upheld the principles of the Society for the Protection of Ancient Buildings. He rebuilt and buttressed the walls where they were unstable, added a handsome two-storey bay to the terrace, to let more light into the late mediaeval wing, and, discreetly away at the north-west corner, built a roughcast service wing which was definitely understated in character and yet just as clearly stated its twentieth-century date. Ashbee said he built in this way "to harmonise and yet not compete with the stonework of the two earlier periods".[3]

By any standards the house is exquisite, a blend of domestic retreat and large working spaces with charming sunny corners both inside and out. The grounds drop away sharply to the south-east, enfolding a cottage, orchard and pond before sloping upward once again to a ridge of huge trees a quarter of a mile to the south. On the west are the kitchen garden, lawn tennis court, rose garden, sunken rock garden and a pool complete with waterfall, while on the south lie a flagged terrace and rolling lawns. Separating these are yew hedges or lavender bushes, favoured by Ethel Coomaraswamy here and in gardens she created elsewhere.

Apart from the structure, many of the timber features inside the house

A modern photograph of the Norman Chapel at Broad Campden, restored and extended by the Guild of Handicraft to a design by C. R. Ashbee in 1905–7

The Guild of Handicraft workshops in Chipping Campden c. 1907, showing the making of the oak lectern for the Norman Chapel. Courtesy of the Campden Trust
Opposite, above: The library at the Norman Chapel at the time the Coomaraswamys lived there, 1907–10. Below: Modern photographs of the Norman Chapel, showing the door to the terrace, door furniture commissioned from craftsmen in Ceylon and a window latch made in the ironsmiths' workshop at the Guild of Handicraft, 1906–7

were made by J. W. Pyment, under whose foremanship the entire work was carried out. The built-in desk, shelves and settle in the library came from his Guild workshop, together with the magnificent dining room door, in the shape of a Gothic arch and inlaid with ebony and pearl to a design by C. R. Ashbee. The casements with their decorative ironwork also came from the Guild workshops, but the door furniture used on the principal doors is damascened ironwork which Coomaraswamy commissioned from Kandyan craftsmen in the mediaeval style; several of the pieces were fine enough to include in the illustrations for *Mediaeval Sinhalese Art*. Rugs and khelims covered the floorboards and Oriental embroideries decorated the walls, creating a rich, textured effect. Woven hangings from Morris & Co. divided off an ''inner sanctum'', the study platform, and a copy of Morris's Kelmscott *Chaucer* was displayed on an oak lectern made at the Guild. Islamic and De Morgan lustre pottery stood along the top of the bookshelves. The room also contained several pieces brought back from Ceylon, among them a magnificent carved chest and a *vina* decorated with incised and painted ivory. The *pièce de résistance* was the piano, the centrepiece for many musical evenings; its woodwork was of Sinhalese origin, with long ornate Guild of Handicraft hinges along the centre fold of the lid.

When the Coomaras moved into the Chapel, the Guild craftsmen were

still at work on it; Philip Mairet, at the time employed in Ashbee's drawing office, writes of looking up from his drawing board to see Ethel Coomara going over design details with her mother-in-law. He noted that, although older than her husband, she was "rather fine", whereas Janet Ashbee described her at this time as a "strange little thin undeveloped figure by day dressed in the gaunt sack-frocks of the Jaeger and Godfrey Blount school [the Healthy and Artistic Dress Union] but at night coming out like a brilliant moth in Eastern plum, cherry and orange colours, with strange Sinhalese jewels."[4]

Two contrasting word portraits of Coomaraswamy exist from this period. The first is an elegant appraisal written by Philip Mairet for his autobiographical papers:

Ananda Kentish Coomaraswamy was of striking appearance; very tall and dark with the olive complexion of his Eurasian ancestry, a shock of jet-black hair, a small moustache and a very little beard in the middle of the chin. There was something leisurely, almost languid about the habitual movements of his long limbs and well-shaped hands, though he could deploy them briskly enough, at tennis or hockey, for example; and his demeanour, normally somewhat aloof and meditative, never lacked decision: it occasionally revealed the undercurrents of a passionate nature. His conversation, though of no special charm or eloquence, was original, often surprising, always gave one the impression of profound thought.[5]

The second description is by Janet Ashbee[6], written on 26 January 1908 after one of the customary social gatherings at the Norman Chapel (often including a talk or lecture) which had become a feature of Campden life. She described Ananda's pale olive skin and thick black hair, his character, "impenetrable and inconsistent", and his "extremely fine and smoothly working mind". "He has been thoroughly spoilt and worshipped by his mother and his wife – and the sweetest nature cannot stand this double strain unwarped." Janet Ashbee goes on to describe them as "like two elves" and admits that she was afraid of Ananda at times, claiming prophetically that she "can trace shreds of the polygamous ancestry that make me shiver and draw back." She ponders on the fact that Ethel is nearly six years older than her thirty-year-old husband, yet "still considers him the youth she knew". She continues: "She has a quick instinct and an intelligence rather of feeling than of brain – fine enthusiasm and great capacity for work – garden, house, music and embroidery." Together the Coomaraswamys were obviously a potent combination: "it was Ethel and Ananda who really *made* the occasion, as they have made the Norman Chapel – I mean its inner life."

Margaret Harwood, Janet Ashbee (standing) and Ethel Coomaraswamy (far right) with children at the bathing lake in Chipping Campden, 20 April 1909. By courtesy of King's College Library, Cambridge. Insets: C. R. Ashbee in 1900, photographed by Frank Lloyd Wright, and Janet Ashbee in 1899, wearing a flowing robe in the style recommended by The Dress Review, *to which she and Ethel Coomaraswamy contributed articles. Both photographs courtesy of Felicity Ashbee*

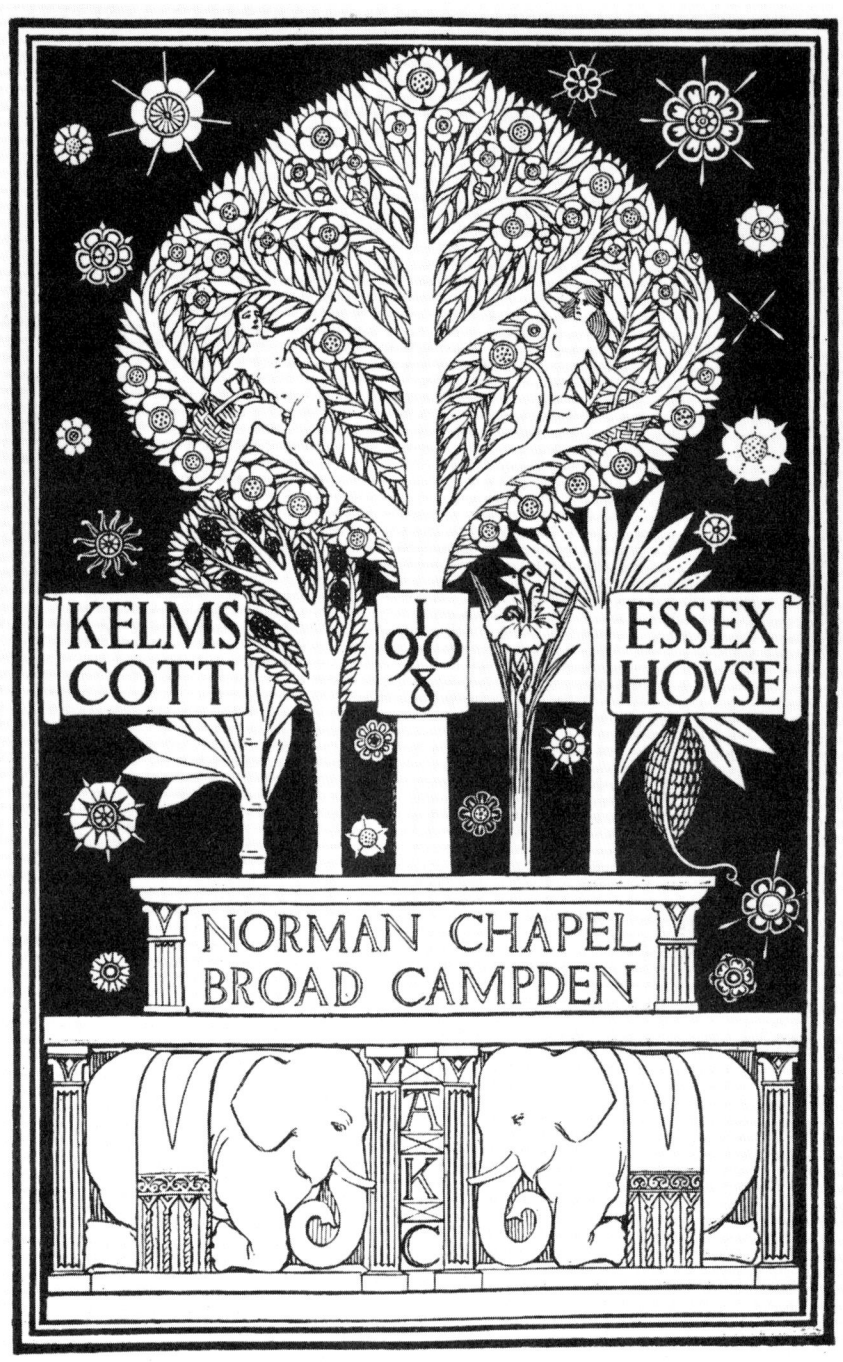

The printer's mark for the Essex House Press, designed by C. R. Ashbee and first used in Mediaeval Sinhalese Art, *printed in 1908*

As well as these activities, plans of the Chapel show that it had a dark-room (unusual for the date) and Ethel no doubt selected images for the book which Ananda was writing in the library above. The preparation of *Mediaeval Sinhalese Art* took fifteen months, including printing which was done on the premises.

On the Coomaraswamys' return to England, the Guild of Handicraft, a multi-disciplinary craft enterprise employing some fifty people and working mostly to commission, was experiencing a severe financial decline which can be directly related to the decision to leave London to partake of the "simple life" in Campden. To try and save the day Ashbee severed various Guild limbs, of which one was the Essex House Press; it used equipment formerly belonging to the Kelmscott Press, which had produced William Morris's legendary *Works of Geoffrey Chaucer* (1896). As well as creating work for the Guild in the shape of the Norman Chapel and its fittings, Ananda Coomaraswamy bought shares in the Guild when they were issued in 1907 and took over the Essex House Press. This enabled him to embark on his distinguished career as an art historian by becoming his own publisher, and at the same time gave him a creative rôle in the Arts and Crafts Movement, which he had so much admired since he first read Morris's writings. He saw to it that the printing of his encyclopaedic work on the minor arts of Ceylon was carried out with imaginative design, within given craft traditions and using high quality materials; the mode was entirely appropriate to the subject.

Ethel Coomaraswamy was by now looking for her own form of expression outside the Ceylonese connection. Her correspondence with Ashbee, then travelling in America, gives some pointers to her views and interests. On 27 November 1908 she wrote that she was going to Bristol, Manchester and Birmingham fighting anti-suffragists, probably at the instigation of her Campden friend Margaret Harwood. In the same letter she reports that Reverend Nason, the vicar from Saintbury, had come to see her with his wife; this is worth noting because in 1912 Ashbee mentioned that they were able to lend a loom or looms for a proposed class at the Guild. Could this meeting in 1908 have led to Ethel Coomaraswamy's first experiments in weaving? The photograph showing her seated at a loom in the Norman Chapel is attributed to 1909–10 but it is not known from where she obtained this, her first loom.

Coomaraswamy returned to India for a brief visit at the beginning of 1909, giving his wife a yellow Persian kitten before he left. A few weeks beforehand Ethel had written to Ashbee: "I am dreading Ananda's going more than I can say. He is very busy now and very impatient to be off. . . .

His capacity for work is enormous, but he has not yet got the art of lecturing and I had to criticise him rather drastically last week at University College.*''[7]

Another letter followed, while Ananda was en route to India:

I am glad you have seen something of the Anglo-Saxon in contact with colour and you can perhaps understand something of the hatred that it stirs up in me when I come across it. . . . A culture that is not of the West is no culture in the eyes of the majority. How impossibly unsympathetic and unimaginative it all is.[8]

At the Norman Chapel there was little to absorb its owner directly. Publication continued at the Essex House Press, albeit of works written almost entirely by Ashbee and Coomaraswamy. Plans for 1909 included Ashbee's *Modern English Silverwork*, which contained some 200 of Philip Mairet's drawings of Ashbee's designs. In 1908 the Press had published Ashbee's *Craftsmanship in Competitive Industry*, which was a justification of the Guild ethic, with a description of its work and social pursuits. Ashbee asserts: ''The Arts and Crafts Movement, if it means anything, means standard whether of work or of life, is the protection of standard, whether in the product or in the producer, and it means these two things must be taken together.''[9]

Here was a code that Ethel Coomaraswamy would follow, or lead in; she frequently spoke of standards or a ''right'' thing, be it in an artefact or an idea, or of ''real feeling''.[10]

No longer conditioned by the movements of her husband, it is very likely that Ethel Coomaraswamy made her first experiments with weaving and dyeing in his ten-month absence. She studied vegetable dyes in the Bodleian Library, Oxford, for her pamphlet (and subsequent book), and she is said to have travelled to the Lake District to learn weaving. No eyewitness accounts support these, save Philip Mairet's oblique mention of research visits ''to several distant counties''[11] in the later period, 1912–15, when he was close to her; only the Guildsman Alec Miller speaks of the learning period in Campden: ''. . . with her botanical knowledge she began learning to dye etc. and set up a loom in the Norman Chapel and began to weave.''[12] Her knowledge of dyes and mordants would certainly have been compounded by that of her father (a chemist) and her husband (a graduate in botany). There is also a reference in the Ashbee Papers to the fact that she began to spin whilst at Campden.

---

*This lecture was in November when Ananda also gave a lecture at the Camberwell School of Art and Crafts, suggested, no doubt, by Fred Partridge who taught silversmithing and jewellery there from April 1907 until 1909. Fred by this time had married May Hart, who taught enamelling at Camberwell from 1905.

Ethel Coomaraswamy making her first experiments in weaving, seated in the music room at the Norman Chapel, 1909–10

CHAPTER 4
"THE REAL AND
THE IDEAL"
1910-1913

At the end of 1909 Ananda returned to Campden and life resumed its normal pace for six months. In the summer of the following year the Coomaraswamys set out together for India (via Munich) to collect works of art for the Indian Society of Oriental Art's United Provinces Exhibition, held in Allahabad in winter 1910–11, leaving Philip Mairet in charge at the Chapel as Ananda's secretary. Ethel Coomaraswamy began the trip enchanted by the places, the buildings and the clothes the people wore (particularly if embroidered). She wrote to the Ashbees and kept a journal which includes some of her rare detailed drawings of textiles and other decorative objects. The journal is rich in detail for those with a taste for travelogues, describing the bazaar, the shops and the street scenes, contrasted with the Englishman's round of visits to the "club" and tea parties. All the while she made notes of Indian textiles, jewellery and accessories; she discusses dyes, draw-room weaving and even breadmaking:

The bazaar was very interesting. Making *daris* in *deshi* or country colours (vegetable colours, colours prepared by the people), blue and white stripes. Much more elaborate *daris* were being made, very fine work. . . . They also make first-class bangles here. Also very nice sort of printed blue cotton sari which is very much worn by the women. Dyeing is also done in indigo.

The shops in the bazaar were beautiful, of stone with stone carved pillars. Men wearing white embroidered shirts with often good buttons – three gold buttons or studs connected with chain.[1]

She bought many things and on 10 August at Shah Dara made a list of the various items she had sent home to Maud in a parcel:

2 blue *namdas*	1 Persian *dari*
1 red one for Lucy James	1 saddle bag ($\frac{1}{2}$ mine)
green cotton material (mine)	1 saddle bag (A's)
1 *dari* (mine)	1 carpet (Mother)[2]

She spent ten days in Calcutta; she visited the School of Art, where she admired the old embroideries, met Sister Nevedita, went to the Tagores (a distinguished family of poets and painters) for breakfast and to Mrs Blount for music; each day was filled with social or artistic engagements, allowing her to steep herself in Indian culture while her husband collected exhibits for the United Provinces Exhibition. But from 11–26 September no entries are made in the journal, an ominous pause.

On 14 September she wrote a sad letter from Allahabad, clothing the

Ethel Coomaraswamy's India Journal for her visit in 1910

break-up of her marriage in the disguise of Ananda wanting to live permanently in India:

I am coming home earlier than I thought; I have a lot to tell you about of a rather sad nature. Ananda has decided he must live out here. He is *really* wanted here and one feels what an influence he is here and that he ought to be here . . . He has a big scheme of a national museum afoot which he hopes will come to something. . . .

But the sad part of it is that the Chapel will have to be given up. I can hardly bring myself to think or write but I can only see that it has to be. On less than £600 a year it is impossible to keep up a house like Norman Chapel *and* a house in India. I feel frightful about it as it means I can't live in Campden. So this is our plan – we had to make one – to let the Chapel semi-furnished for say 5 or 7 years' lease, for me to build a small cottage (£500) at Saunton, the only other place I could live besides Campden, or rather, want to live, and to live there when not in India. Probably I shall not go to India at all. When one is married to a very alive person like Ananda one has to take the chance of these uprootings! But it tears one's soul to shreds sometimes. But the Saunton cottage idea compensates for a lot; as I love the place and you will all be able to come and stay with me and bathe all day long!

I have already written about the land. It has always been my dream to have a cottage at Saunton but we had hoped as a sort of supplement to the Chapel. I will send you a plan of it. You must let me talk it over with you. I can't have an architect so don't have hopes![3]

She adds that she plans to take out all the small furniture, to leave the large pieces and the piano and to sell the press: ''Only Margaret [Harwood] knows about this.''

The truth was that Ananda had fallen in love some months before with a young musician called Alice Richardson, a former art school friend of Philip Mairet's who had visited them in Campden. Wanting heirs, he is said to have proposed a polygamous relationship which his wife could not countenance.

Ethel Coomaraswamy sailed home aboard the *Nera* from Bombay on 3rd October; she was in her 38th year. On the return voyage she wrote of ''six days of misery, feeling all nose and stomach''.[4]

In January and February 1911 she languished in Saunton, near Barnstaple, staying at a guest house by the sea. Her letters are painful; she writes to Ashbee:

I have never wanted you and Janet so much as I have this last week and shall want. Why do you go and get ill when you are wanted so badly here? . . . for a woman to keep herself ''efficient'' and of some use in the world, she must have men who can understand and sympathise that she can go to to be understood. . . .

As for myself, I am nearing the seventh hell. I am just making up my mind that I have to go and tell Lady C that her son doesn't want to live with me any more, and it is a little difficult business for an individual to do with such proud instincts as I have but it's got to be done and I'm not going to lie any more about it. Charley, it's very difficult for me to reconcile myself to being thrown aside and I don't like it. But thank goodness I can still love as much and more than ever I did. . . .

I can't live in Campden without A, and I can't live in London because it's such a hell, but what am I to do? My brain does not seem capable of conceiving a future. What an aimless individual is a woman without a cause. Well, if I had not you as a friend whom I have idealised into one of the most wonderful people in the world, I should be a few grades lower in the Purgatory than I am. But please note this – I am intellectually convinced that the real and the ideal are very far apart.[5]

After a letter of 28 March 1911, congratulating the Ashbees on the birth of their first child, no more correspondence was exchanged between them until the following December, when Ethel asks if they can forgive each other. Bitterness, maybe combined with jealousy over the arrival of a baby, seems to have caused a break with the Ashbees as well as with Ananda.

Despite depression and even a threat of suicide, in the year that lay ahead Ethel Coomaraswamy had to dismantle the Norman Chapel and rebuild her life; her sense of disappointment must have been intense but, as she wrote later, she was satisfied in the knowledge that she had never been deceived. The kindness and helpfulness of Philip Mairet during this period did much to ease the situation; he worked with her on clearing the Chapel (almost everything connected with India and Ceylon was stored for Ananda Coomaraswamy) and advised her on design details for the bungalow she was building at Saunton Sands. This building project was a powerful force in her recovery; it represented a long-held ideal and stretched her own creative energy. The craft of weaving would present an extension to this challenge.

She lived in a rented bungalow from May 1911 to Spring 1912 while Broadlys was being built. The design was taken partly from the home of Mrs Cardew (the mother of potter Michael Cardew) and, no doubt, partly from ideas formed in Ceylon; the bungalow as an architectural form was not yet common in England. Philip Mairet wrote of the plan:

My architectural services were negligible. Mrs Coomara had sketched out a plan of what she wanted and left the rest to the local builder who happened to be worthy of her innocent trust in him; she probably supposed that I, a mere draughtsman in Ashbee's office, knew more about building than I did. I had nothing to teach the builder anyway; and my kind hostess seemed more interested in giving me a good holiday.[6]

Broadlys, the bungalow built by Ethel Coomaraswamy at Saunton Sands near Braunton in Devon, where she lived in 1912 and 1913; she and Philip Mairet can be seen seated on the terrace overlooking the sea

Built on a plot of sand dune measuring about an acre square, Broadlys has large metal casements (a pair of which form an unusual right-angled corner) giving wide vistas of the sea and dunes, plain walls and doors, iron door latches, brick fireplaces, and a built-in dresser and cupboards. One of the front rooms originally had a fixture along one wall which is thought to have been used for hanging yarns and lengths of cloth. More curious is the arrangement of small iron studs in the plain oak doors; the carpenter who put them in as a boy apprentice used to relate the following: "The big black man pinned a paper near each door showing the position of the studs and said 'Boy, copy that correctly, it won't mean anything to you but it's a symbol and means a lot to me.'"[7]

This vivid image seems to confirm that Coomaraswamy visited Broadly's when the building was nearing completion, which coincided with his return to England in 1912; he most certainly paid for it to be built and, in addition, made over some investments to Ethelmary. (Henceforward she requested that her two Christian names were used as one, although to many people she remained "Ethel".)

Broadlys was completed early in 1912, and she lived there for a little over a year, after which it was used by her family for holidays until about 1931. Janet Ashbee went to stay in February and wrote to C.R.A. (as he liked to be called):

Dear Lad,

It is all right and everything has come round as it was in the beginning. Ethel is looking very well, and is heroically cheerful and very busy weaving the most lovely stuffs. . . .

This little house is just as perfect as all Ethel's creations and has that wonderful sense of *well-being* and beauty that she carries about with her . . . like the Chapel only in miniature and without the oldness. [Of the view] . . . nothing for about twenty miles except bents and sandy hillocks and the enormous stretch of Barnstaple bay with miles of white breakers roaring. It is very desolate and very beautiful. . . .

She says she cannot stand another winter here by herself but has no plans. . . . She is coming to Margaret's in May for the whole summer and wants to set up her loom at the Guild – a very good idea I think. The whole thing is most awfully pathetic and heartrending. She has been doing a lot of reading and going for a good deal of "advanced" feminist literature. We have not come to grips with anything yet, but only gossipped. She can hardly bear to talk about Broad Campden, or the Chapel (which she puts on one side as "nothing to do with her") or Baby – but is much more her old self than I remember her for two or three years.[8]

Ethelmary therefore decided to move and to set up her weaving workshop in earnest, and in 1912–13 she found The Thatched House in Shottery near Stratford-on-Avon.

Philip Mairet's rôle, from the time of his first visit to Saunton in 1911, had meanwhile changed from one of friend and confidant to that of lover and, after the Coomaraswamys' decree nisi was granted, eventually to that of husband. Their first "contract" in Oxford was charmingly original; a document was drafted and inscribed with Indian ink on vellum. Although the marriage was looked upon with suspicion by friends such as Ashbee, it went ahead in May 1913, when Ethelmary was aged 42 and Philip 27:

The nuptial meeting was in the "city of dreaming spires"; the ceremony on the bank of the Isis, a little above Magdalen Bridge. Alec Miller and a Mrs Evans, a friend of Ethelmary's, signed their names after ours upon the scroll of vellum. We lunched modestly in the High Street (the restaurant was as 'unlicensed' as the rite we had just performed), and then we parted from our witnesses, mounted our bicycles and rode off to the west. For a week or more we toured the countryside, visiting numerous churches, lodging each night at a different town or village and picnicking by the wayside, until we reached the home that Ethelmary had established near Stratford-on-Avon. But before this blissful honeymoon was half over,

A family group at Broadlys in 1912 or 1913. Left to right: Maud Partridge, her mother Mary, Philip Mairet, Ethel Coomaraswamy, Fred Partridge, his wife May Hart Partridge, their daughter Joan and James Partridge

the curious document we had so lately signed appeared to us in quite another light. Was it worth while, after all, to refuse to drop that pinch of incense on the altar of Caesar? We were now facing the facts of our situation; eagerly discussing our domestic arrangements, furnishings, the outhouse that was to be my studio and workshop and all the fascinating paraphernalia needed to set up as independent craftsmen. To register our union would be a cheap insurance against indubitable embarrassments and possible handicaps to our ambitions.

So Ethelmary paid a visit to London (where I went on working three days a week; the rest of the time at home), and I left the studio in Great Ormond Street on the first stroke of the lunch interval, to meet my bride at the registry office at a quarter past one. With George Chettle and Fred Partridge as witnesses, I wedded my wife again with the pale gold ring made for me at Campden. This took about twenty minutes. Our meal at the vegetarian restaurant in New Oxford Street (three courses, at sixpence a head and very nourishing too) was despatched in time for me to be back at my easel only a few minutes late.

From the amateur *rîte de passage* by the sunlit Isis where we had exchanged our formal vows, to the sordid surroundings in which they acquired legal warrant was a mortifying descent to the practical. It did not make our union any more of a real marriage in the absolute sense I would now attach to the word, nor make it more durable. But in the circumstances it was a return to reason.[9]

CHAPTER 5
"A RETURN TO REASON"
1913-1917

The short spell living and working at The Thatched House in Shottery provided a base for Ethel Mairet to consolidate her first weaving workshop.

The house, which was leased, had been run since about 1910 as a tapestry studio; it is likely that the yarns, looms and other equipment were taken over by the Mairets with the house. Apart from some rudimentary lessons in Ceylon and the British Isles, Ethel Mairet was self-taught as a weaver, spinner and dyer. Her knowledge of technique was elementary, but her sense of colour and yarn quality were reasonably highly developed thanks to her experience in embroidery and her critical eye. Her first weavings had probably been in tapestry technique on an upright loom, or in plain weave on a flat loom; early photographs exist of her working in both methods, but there are no artefacts surviving from that period. The earliest documentation of her sustained activity is an invitation card for an exhibition at The Thatched House. The three other exhibitors were Wentworth Huyshe (decorative paintings) and William Mark (enamelling), both of the Guild connection, and W. Fishley Holland (earthenware pottery) from Clevedon, Somerset.

Philip Mairet describes the "weaving business" as flourishing and not short of assistants; four apprentices are recorded and, judging by the size of the house, this was all that could be accommodated. The first two were young girls, Rita Hawkes and Kathleen Heron, who were joined in late 1916 or early 1917 by Elizabeth Peacock, then aged 37, and Dorothy Moore. As far as we know, none of them had had any previous knowledge of weaving but three of them went on to found their own workshops and earn their

Elizabeth Peacock demonstrating spinning at an exhibition, 1917–20

living from the craft. Kathleen Heron, Rita Hawkes and Dorothy Moore parted company with Ethel Mairet when she left Shottery in 1918, but Elizabeth Peacock moved with the workshop to its permanent site in Ditchling.

Little is known about the type and quality of the weavings produced at Shottery; only a pinafore dress and cap, woven in wool and trimmed with hand-woven braid, have survived. It is likely that Elizabeth Peacock's aptitude in hand-spinning was exploited and that the yarn (mainly wool) was woven into simple rugs, blankets and scarves with stripes or inlay patterns at the ends. The subject of vegetable dyeing (colours obtained from organic matter) was uppermost in Ethel Mairet's mind; she experimented and read widely on the subject, and in 1915 she wrote a pamphlet "The Future of Dyeing"[1] which was revised, printed and published as a delightful and unassuming little volume, *A Book on Vegetable Dyes*, the following year by Douglas (known as Hilary) Pepler at the Hampshire House Press in Hammersmith, London.

Here it may be useful to set Ethel Mairet in context as a weaver. During

A BOOK ON
VEGETABLE
DYES

BY
ETHEL M. MAIRET

A.D.   1916

PUBLISHED BY DOUGLAS PEPLER
AT THE HAMPSHIRE HOUSE
WORKSHOPS HAMMERSMITH W

The title page for A Book on Vegetable Dyes, *written by Ethel Mairet and printed by Douglas Pepler at the Hampshire House Workshops in 1916; he considered this title page the best he had ever composed. Presented to the Crafts Study Centre by Joyce Griffiths*

the nineteenth century the tradition of hand-weaving had almost completely died out in Britain; only a few outposts survived in rural areas, mainly in the Outer Hebrides, the home of Harris tweed, and some regions of Ireland and Wales. Ethel Mairet may well have seen Harris tweed being woven; photographic negatives, recently discovered in Campden, show that Ananda Coomaraswamy travelled to north-west Scotland shortly after their marriage in July 1902 and it is likely that his wife accompanied him. The hand-spun and vegetable-dyed cloth would have impressed her.

Silk weaving endured in Spitalfields until about 1910 and it had been with the help of an old Spitalfields weaver that William Morris had set up his hand-operated jacquard loom in the 1870s, on which he produced heavy woollen furnishings at his workshops in Merton. Morris had also set up carpet-weaving frames at Hammersmith in 1878 and in the same year devised and set up a tapestry loom in his bedroom, on which he wove his "Cabbage and Vine" design. From 1881, Morris and Co. produced tapestries at Merton Abbey and, although Burne-Jones was responsible for many of the designs, the revival of the art was due to Morris's initiative (described as one of his "greatest triumphs"[2] by the historian Paul Thompson).

The Guild of Handicraft had no textiles section, but this does not mean that hand-weaving was not practised in crafts revival circles; it was, by 1900, being revived by many individuals but mostly in the form of pattern weaving and tapestry. Tapestry weaving flourished in several small and rather self-conscious workshops, such as Ickleford Art Industries and the Peasant Arts Society in Haslemere. *The Studio* of 1907 covered the revival of handicraft at Haslemere, which was attributable to the activities of Godfrey and Mrs Blount, who also ran the London depot of the Peasant Arts Society, and Mr and Mrs Joseph King. (The Blounts were associated with *The Dress Review*, to which Ethel Mairet contributed articles.) The Kings owned a weaving workshop for domestic linens, the Haslemere Weaving Industry, and Edmund and Nero Hunter operated the St Edmundsbury Silk Weaving Works, using jacquard looms; in 1907 they moved into spacious new premises in Letchworth. Also associated with this group was Luther Hooper, known for his draw-loom woven damasks and brocades. His manual *Hand-Loom Weaving*, published in 1910, is still in use today and played a major part in popularising weaving. In the preface, Hooper claimed that hand-loom weaving had not entirely died out and that handicraft societies were flourishing, but at the same time he alleges that no real advance in weaving had taken place for a hundred years and that the invention of the jacquard loom, with its multiplication of patterns, was responsible for the separation of the art of designing from the craft of weaving.

A typical example of the woven textile designs produced by Morris & Co., Henry Dearle's design "Helena" (1891), woven wool and silk doublecloth. Crown Copyright Victoria and Albert Museum

It is against this background that Ethel Mairet's workshop, and those of her first pupils, must be set and their conscious return to the production of simple cloth evaluated. Her work, begun at Shottery and continued at Gospels in Ditchling, represents a move away from pictorial weaving to the exploration of surface qualities inherent in the yarn's character.

Life at Shottery was full: Philip travelled to London for two or three days a week where he was employed as a draughtsman in a stained glass workshop, returning home to continue this work in his studio, making both cartoons and actual pieces of fired glass. In London he lodged with Fred and May Partridge who lived in Great Ormond Street and ran a jewellery and enamelling workshop in Dean Street. He and Ethelmary enjoyed both their chosen crafts and their leisure, in particular the performances of the Frank Benson theatre company at Stratford and the folk music of Cecil Sharp, whom they were to get to know well.

The outbreak of war in 1914 cast a depressing note, but it was overshadowed by Philip's reaction when he proudly showed his wife his first complete panel of stained glass; her criticism was acid, she "found fault with the whole design"[3] and reduced him to a state of humiliation. From then on Philip began to seek inspiration from someone other than Ethelmary, and he found it in Dmitri Mitrinovic, a charismatic Serbian poet and social commentator attached to the Serbian Legation in London. They had recently met at the Victoria and Albert Museum, at an exhibition of sculpture by the Serbian Mestrovic. During 1916 and 1917 Philip was mostly in France on Red Cross work, but at every opportunity when passing through London he met Mitrinovic who schooled him in philosophy by lengthy discussion and the loan of esoteric literature. Philip Mairet was one of several protegés for whom Mitrinovic devised spiritual programmes, based on his personal doctrine of pan-humanism. A description of Mitrinovic, written by Paul Selver, shows his charisma:

He did, in fact, possess many of the attributes with which novelists of the Guy Boothby breed (no disparagement is implied here) equip mystery men from the Near East who form the centre of a tangled plot. Yes, Mitrinovic outwardly fulfilled all the requirements in this respect, with his shaven head, his swarthiness, his dark garments and his hypnotic eyes. This latter item must not be dismissed as a hackneyed flourish. Hardly had I shaken hands with him than I found myself so affected by his mere presence that I nearly lost consciousness. This had never before happened to me, nor did it ever happen again. . . . Amid the uncertainties that blur the image of Mitrinovic the man, I can bear witness to the fact that he was both accomplished and erudite. He spoke a choicely worded English, to which he imparted a solemn and musical intonation. Evidence of his wide reading and critical discernment asserted itself casually in the course of conversation.[4]

Philip returned home from France for Christmas 1916 and Ethel Mairet organised a family gathering at Shottery. Shortly afterwards she and Philip made their first visit to Ditchling at the invitation of Douglas Pepler. There they met other craftsmen who had recently moved to the village: the calligrapher Edward Johnston and the sculptor Eric Gill, in the middle of whose birthday party they coincidentally arrived. With its strong overtones of the old Guild of Handicraft days, this was the kind of society which the Mairets would have wished to join and it was Philip Mairet's good fortune to be offered a job on Pepler's farm. Ethel Mairet was to uproot and move yet again.

The next Partridge family gathering was at Easter 1917; it should have been a happy occasion. Several of the family were out walking, leaving Ethel Mairet and May Hart Partridge at home. Ethel prepared tea and went to call May, only to see, through an internal window off the staircase, her body hanging from a beam. She rushed from the house and returned with a "labouring man" from nearby, but they cut the body down to find her dead. Janet Ashbee, hearing of the tragedy, immediately wrote to C.R.A.:

Isn't it awful how Ethel draws these things unto her "as with a cartrope". [She could not have chosen a more unsuitable metaphor.] It couldn't have happened to anyone but Ethel. Meantime Fred turned up and spent the night crying with remorse and guilty misery – it appears he really had never "loved" her and her jealous and spaniel-like adoration of him had driven him to a frenzy of repulsion tempered by bouts of "attentions" and attempts at amity. . . .

Ditchling village in the 1920s, from a contemporary postcard

Poor Ethel and PAM, who mercifully returned two days later from Ditchling where he is ploughing Douglas Pepler's land, feel now that their house is haunted, and Ethel sees the pendent figure everywhere like ''Thrawn Janet'' suspended by her nail, by a thread of scarlet wool. It now turns out May used often to threaten suicide, in her jealous cat-like rages, but no one took her seriously. It was a bit of old rope she had found in the weaving room.[5]

Fred Partridge was devastated; he told Janet that May had ''tried to possess him body, soul and spirit''.[6] Ethelmary was to ''adopt'' his daughter Joan: ''But the Harts don't relish it. They have always thought us dangerous people.''[7]

The ''dangerous people'' were shortly to move to Ditchling, and by November 1917 the Mairets were negotiating for a plot of land on which to build.

CHAPTER 6
THE MOVE TO
DITCHLING
1917-1920

Gospels, Ethel Mairet's home and workshop in Ditchling, was her third and last building project. A prolonged correspondence with her solicitor, Walter Bartlett, which show signs of irritability on both sides, gives a full account of the negotiations. By 21 December 1918 the plots known as Gunt's Field had been secured; they lay to the south of the village, adjacent to Gospels Farm which was at that time leased to Molly Stobart. Between May and August 1918 negotiations over an additional purchase, that of Sundown Cottage, ensued. Ethel Mairet obviously intended to move into the cottage so that she could oversee the building work at Gunt's Field; meanwhile Philip Mairet was no longer working on the land in Ditchling but was in Wakefield Prison, the result of his stand during the War as a conscientious objector. From 1917 bills for building materials (for the most part ordered direct from the suppliers by Ethel Mairet) started to appear and 45,000 bricks were delivered from Norwood's Brickworks at Plumpton, a few miles from Ditchling. The builder, Harry Grainger from Brighton, did not begin work, however, until long after the conveyancing was completed; the bills show that he first of all carried out alterations to Sundown Cottage before starting work on the new house in 1919.

No records exist of a design for Gospels. George Chettle (formerly a draughtsman in Ashbee's office and Philip Mairet's art school friend) has been suggested as its architect, but this has recently been refuted. It seems most likely that Ethel Mairet herself produced a sketch plan and that this, possibly augmented by details designed by Philip Mairet, was followed by the builder.

Gospels, Ditchling, built by Ethel Mairet in 1919–20; this view shows the outside of the weaving room

Gospels is built in the "Ditchling vernacular" of brick construction, half hung with tiles, with white-painted horizontal casements. It has many striking features, and anyone who has visited both can see that some of them are derived from the Norman Chapel. The house is dominated by the "big weaving room", a double-height space of proportions similar to the Chapel itself, with a staircase leading to a wide timber balcony at the western end. Instead of a round-headed window (as in the chancel arch at the Norman Chapel) there is an oriel at balcony level, and formerly there were a pair of double doors beneath it at ground level, through which looms could be brought without having to be dismantled. Windows light the room all along the south (garden) side, one of them reaching the full height of the wall to finish under the eaves. In Ethel Mairet's day the room was heated by means of a fat-bellied cast-iron stove and a brick fireplace.

Next to the weaving room was Ethel Mairet's office and running at right angles to the work area was the domestic wing of the buildings; the house

The dyehouse yard at Gospels; an underground cistern supplied rainwater for dyeing

contained six bedrooms. Throughout the house the Arts and Crafts idiom is evident: oak exterior doors were supplied by Ernest Gimson working at Sapperton in the Cotswolds, nine ash doors were ordered from Harry Slee of Braunton in North Devon and a pair of deal doors and casement stays came from J. W. Pyment (formerly of the Guild) in Campden. The paving tiles, called "red gins", came from the firm of E. and R. Norman of Chailey in Sussex.

The one item of furniture which can definitely be associated with the Mairets' move to Ditchling is an oak refectory table made by George Romney Green; its shape and size recall the library table in the Norman Chapel, laden with books. Outside, Eric Gill cut the date July 1919 on the foundation

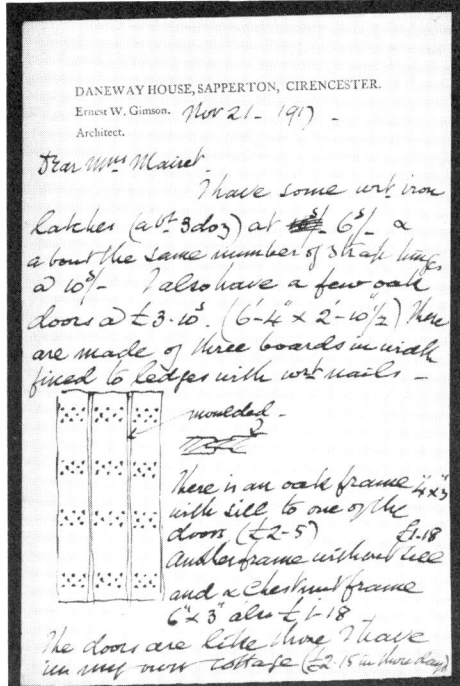

A letter from Ernest Gimson in 1917, when Ethel Mairet was planning Gospels

The front door at Gospels, made by Ernest Gimson in oak with wrought iron nails

stone; he also made the splendid oak sign, "Ethel Mairet, weaver and dyer", adorned with a madder plant, which once hung near the front door.

Alongside the main building was the dye house, probably a converted farm building; here a long brick hearth or trough contained a log fire on which up to six dye baths could be heated at once. The water used for dyeing was hand-pumped from a specially constructed underground cistern in the yard, into which rainwater drained from the roofs. The yard was an essential work area, and from it a wooden stairway led to a garret above the dye house where yarns and fleece were stored.

Undaunted by the mood of upheaval, Ethel Mairet completed one new piece of writing, "An Essay on Crafts and Obedience", (1918) and oversaw the production of the second edition of *A Book on Vegetable Dyes* (1917), both published by Douglas Pepler at St Dominic's Press in Ditchling.

Early editions of the dyebook, as it is always known, have a seven-page introduction on the philosophy of natural dyeing. In it the author praises the vegetable dyes of primitive cultures, in contrast to which she deplores

Craftsmen-made doors and latches at Gospels
Opposite: This stone garden roller was given to Ethel and Philip Mairet by Eric Gill in 1920.
The inscription reads "Come all you false young men, do not leave me here to complain"

THIS essay is meant for those who intend to work with their hands at any craft.   Its subject is the serious and fundamental necessity of hand work as an essential function of the life of man.

A small body of craftsmen is now holding its own with difficulty against the tremendous forces of commercialism which have organized the produc–

The opening lines of "An Essay on Crafts and Obedience", the pamphlet written jointly by Ethel and P. A. Mairet and printed by Douglas Pepler at Ditchling in 1918. The woodcut for the initial letter was very probably designed by Eric Gill

"hideous aniline colours" and the "recent fashion for muddy art colours".[1] She acknowledges the contribution of the Futurists:

We are now emerging from mud colours, as I would call them, to the period of the brilliant colouring of the Futurist. Here we have the scientific colouring used with real skill. The Futurist has perhaps indicated a possible way in which chemical colours may be used by the artist and is teaching people the value of simple combinations of brilliant colours.[2] [The Italian Futurists had held an exhibition in London in 1912 and it is possibly the paintings of Boccioni and Severini which are referred to.]

A passage further on echoes her frequent claim, so reminiscent of Morris:

The aim of commerce is material gain; the aim of the crafts is to make life, and no trouble must be spared to reach that end. It must always be before the craft worker. Dyeing is an art; the moment science dominates it, it is an art no longer, and the craftsman must go back to the time before science touched it, and begin all over again.[3]

The first and second editions of the dyebook also contain a sonorous little publisher's note by Douglas Pepler. It ends:

In view of the beginning [a quotation from the Book of Genesis on the goodness of making] it is desirable to record what still survives of the traditions of making good things; and I shall endeavour to publish the instructions and advice of men and women who still follow these good traditions.[4]

"An Essay on Crafts and Obedience", although written jointly by Ethel and Philip Mairet and described by him as "the product of a red-hot wrangling collaboration",[5] contains ideas which can clearly be attributed to each of them. The main contention, abstract and idealistic, is surely Philip's, perhaps tinged with a touch of Ananda Coomaraswamy's mysticism; it is that the crafts in Britain have no spiritual centre.

No compelling universal form, no creative Spirit of this Age is using us and speaking in our work. We have lost the sense of work, of craftsmanship which is in obedience and praise to God and in the service of humankind.

The great characteristic of every period of good art and craftsmanship is a general unity of inspiration. India, Egypt, Greece, Italy, medieval Europe – each of these in its time of greatness unified all its arts and crafts into one great beauty; the same spirit shone through every craft. . . .

At every period when art was great, there was a great religious interpretation of the meaning and nature of life. There was a unifying spirit which bound all together and formed, as it were, a common language. It is this which is needed before the gift of universal beauty will again permeate our work.[6]

His enlargement of the theme implies that at that time he himself felt the need for a leader or an ideal to serve and follow; in his formative years he had been influenced in turn by C. R. Ashbee, Ananda Coomaraswamy, and, most importantly, Mitrinovic. Ethel Mairet, one feels, merely "strung along" with this view of the crafts; there is no separate instance of her ever having expanded on it. Her own dogma emerges later in the essay, where she talks of the study and teaching of craft and the wish to restore the "conditions of the workshop tradition":

Most artist-craftsmen have served no real apprenticeship, but have come to the study of their craft by the study of art. We owe more to travel, museums, private study and technical books than to intimacy with past masters of our work; and most craftsmen are now agreed that this is a disadvantage. We need this living, oral and practical continuity of education. Our workshops must become schools of workmanship, producing good workers as well as good work. But it is objected, we cannot teach in this true historical and living way because we have not been so taught ourselves. We have had to pick up the broken threads of tradition from everywhere as individuals, and we know things intellectually rather than by natural growth. This is true, but there is no other way by which we ourselves can begin to restore the conditions of workshop tradition. We must not merely praise the old training by apprenticeship, but take and teach apprentices. And we must teach unstintingly all we have learnt or can learn ourselves. Nor need we despise the modern methods by which we have learnt. If we have learnt from books and museums, have studied from ancient work and peasant traditions in all parts of the world, let us teach it in all our workshops. . . .

In all great periods of workmanship the craft has been a mystery, the learning of it a kind of initiation requiring long probation, obedience and devotion. This is a most difficult thing to demand of those we teach. We have not the monopoly of knowledge that the old masters had, and our workshops cannot have the same rigidity nor the paternal authority of the master craftsman as they would have in the midst of a well established tradition. But *tradition is a living force* and we must be fully conscious that we are building tradition, each workshop will add some thing to it, each pupil will add something. To work at a craft means steady and concentrated work. It cannot be done by a few lessons in a workshop or an Art School.[7]

Ethel Mairet's contribution can be seen as justifying her own untrained background, and at the same time laying down a framework for her workshop of the twenties.

The publication of the essay also served as an initiation ceremony into the Ditchling group of craftsmen. Pepler, Gill and the others had no hesitation in publishing their own thoughts and ditties, and they obviously encouraged others to do the same. "The Song of the Evening", composed by Philip Mairet in 1918 to celebrate the second anniversary of the Ditchling Press, sets the scene very well. Here are two of the twelve verses, sung to a tune from Cecil Sharp's *Sea Chanties*:

> We bought a case of Caslon Primer
> *Way Ho, a-printing we will go.*
> And set up a press in the village of Ditchling,
> As the old printers printed printing long ago.

> We did a book on dyeing rightly,
> *Way Ho, a-dyeing we will go.*
> That taught the art of dyeing brightly,
> As the old dyers dyed their dyeing long ago.

The Mairets' collaboration over the pamphlet, uniting the visionary and the practical view of crafts, could have been the perfect foundation for a working and a personal relationship; indeed it probably was, for a couple of years, until Philip Mairet was seduced out of this microcosmic village society into a world infinitely more various and complex.

CHAPTER 7
THE WORKSHOP AT
GOSPELS
1920-1930

Once Gospels was completed, towards the end of 1920, Ethel Mairet could begin in earnest to create her workshop and its apprenticeship system. Hitherto she had been dogged by family affairs and the loss of her first and most reliable worker, Elizabeth Peacock, who left to join forces with Molly Stobart, a smallholder, taking many of Ethel Mairet's clients with her. Although, in the words of the teacher and weaver Ella McLeod, "the courtesies were strictly maintained", the situation was exacerbated when Peacock set up her own workshop in the Ditchling locality in 1922.

Stresses of a personal nature included the removal of the entire Partridge family to Ditchling. Old Mrs Partridge and Maud rented Sopers (the Gills' first Ditchling house) and Fred and his second wife Nellie lived there too until Ethel Mairet vacated Sundown Cottage, when they took it on and ran it as a tearoom. Fred worked in an upper room at Sundown Cottage, by now making wooden as well as metal items. He and Nellie separated about 1927, and Maud took control of the tearoom. Fred's partially sighted child Joan also lived at Sopers until 1920–21, when she too moved to Gospels to be brought up under the Mairets' care.

Joan Partridge recalls that rows between her aunt and uncle began about six months after she started living with them. Philip Mairet would often leave Ethel Mairet alone in order to see Mitrinovic, his spiritual mentor: "She suffered but she let him go his own sweet way."[1]

Joan Partridge recalls that although her aunt "was not particularly fond of children" she was a very charitable person, whereas her own parents, whom she had never lived with but only seen for short holidays, "were not fit to bring up a child". She was sent to see her father daily "under pressure", but the bonus of seeing her Aunt Maud was a consolation. The relationship between Ethel Mairet and Joan has been described by Petra Gill (now Petra Tegetmeier), daughter of Eric Gill and an apprentice at Gospels in the early years:

It was rather a sad relationship I always thought, because Ethel Mairet was so full of vitality herself and she hadn't got a lot of sympathy with people who were a bit handicapped in some way, I imagine. I think she used to get rather impatient with Philip Mairet because he had this dreadful stammer at one time and I think that used to rather frustrate her.[2]

Joan Partridge's comments on her aunt and uncle's relationship are borne out by the fragmented nature of Philip Mairet's life in the early twenties. He did not resume stained glass work, but began to write contributions to the literary and philosophical journal *The New Age* and in 1922 he joined the Old Vic Company as an actor, making use of talents discovered in the Guild of Handicraft annual plays. On stage his normally marked stammer completely disappeared. At weekends he brought home from London groups of actors and other friends, among them Geoffrey Clark of

The potter Shoji Hamada visited Ethel Mairet with Bernard Leach in 1921 and wrote to her on his return to Japan

the BBC, Valerie Cooper, who ran a school of eurythmics and dance, and, occasionally, the more intellectual Mitrinovic with disciples such as Helen Soden, who later settled in Ditchling. These colourful guests attracted comment in the village; there were country dancing parties at Gospels, to music played by a pupil of Cecil Sharp. The twenties was a period of weekend parties, of discussions and lectures, musical evenings and impromptu acting; twenty people or more would fill the big weaving room "from Ditchling and from away, the Christies and all sorts of people. They would play and sing; at Christmas parties we had games and all sorts of fun!"[3]

Among the people who visited Gospels were other craftsmen from outside the Ditchling circle. Bernard Leach and Shoji Hamada, who in 1920 had established a pottery at St Ives in Cornwall, came to see her the following year, 1921. Both men much admired her work and the value she placed on the quality of life. Hamada recalled the occasion in the collection of his memoirs made by Bernard Leach in 1975:

When Leach and I visited Mrs Mairet, the mother of English hand-weaving, in Ditchling, Sussex, she served us dinner using a complete set of slipware, which I have never forgotten. The dishes were products of Fishley, a potter who preserved the good traditions of England, the last one to do so. His slipware was often put on display in the market and sold there. The large and small pitchers, oval dishes and green plates all went well with the large oak table. When you are invited to dinner by someone, you often notice, as a potter, that dishes of lower quality are used together with superior pieces. But Mrs Mairet served food on the best dishes, a perfect score.[4]

During the same visit Ethel Mairet gave Hamada a hand-woven suit. He had asked to buy a length of cloth, but as none was available she gave him a suit which had been recently made for her husband. Hamada can be seen wearing it in numerous photographs of the period, and by way of acknowledgement he sent her a present from Japan and returned to see her on his visit to England in 1929. Hamada also made plans for her work to be exhibited with that of Bernard Leach and William Staite-Murray in the Kyū-kyo-dō Gallery in Tokyo but it is not known what was included.

The effect which Ethel Mairet's work had on Hamada and on the Japanese crafts is described by Janet Leach:

Mr Hamada and Dr Soetsu Yanagi came to England in 1929. It was Dr Yanagi's first visit. One of their main stops was Ditchling. I know for a fact that it was through this connection that Dr Yanagi and Hamada introduced vegetable-dyed homespun wool into Japan. Schools and classes of it are still going on today. When I first arrived in Japan in 1954 I was amused to see that every male member of the

Japanese Folkcraft Movement could be identified by their fuzzy-wuzzy neckties in the home-spun manner. Knowing that Japan did not have any sheep I enquired about this and was given these facts.[5]

Bernard Leach also returned to Ditchling, living in a caravan in 1936 while he was preparing *A Potter's Book*.

This busy social life was part of the general mood of post-war relief and optimism against which the Gospels workshop was framed. From the early twenties Ethel Mairet took apprentices, each staying not less than two years unless they were over twenty, in which case they usually stayed eighteen months; a total of seventeen apprentices are recorded for the decade. Some of them paid a premium to join the workshop, but most were paid a small wage: those under twenty earned 10 shillings a week for the first six or nine months, graduating to 15 shillings and finally to £1 a week. Kitty Doncaster, an apprentice between 1922 and 1924, wrote to the weaver Alice Hindson on the subject in 1948:

We just did any work that came along, we were supposed to start with spinning but actually we were soon on the looms and of course doing dyeing as well. We worked a seven-hour day and had Saturday afternoons off. Mrs Mairet was good about days off, holidays, and the whole arrangement fairly elastic. At that time she had about half a dozen of us in the weaving room but I believe subsequently decided that it would be better not to have so many youngsters together.[6]

Petra Tegetmeier has also described the terms on which apprentices were employed:

Now Eileen [Baker], I don't think she paid a premium, I think Mrs M paid her. She paid me half a crown, she didn't give it to me regularly, I used to have to ask her; after a month you used to go and ask for ten shillings. And of course you could always get material from her, she was so generous that way. If you wanted anything like a length of material you could always buy it very reasonably from her. . . . In fact I have no complaints against her at all. I think she used to find me pretty stupid about adding up the percentages and things but she never said. When you were making up your lengths of cloth you always had to have it calculated up to the half yard. I always used to get very muddled as to how much I had taken off the warp. She was very patient.[7]

The "youngsters" were for the most part "gentlewomen under no particular pressure to earn a living"[8] (only three were men) and, though perhaps not the backbone of production, they were certainly Ethel Mairet's strongest supporters, for the work of Gospels spread by word of mouth in artistic circles. For many of them this was a new experience both in lifestyle and

Staff and apprentices at Gospels in 1923–4. Standing, left to right: Dorothea Wilkinson, Maud Partridge, Elsie Harbour. Centre: Grace Parker, Eileen Baker, unknown. Front: Millie Gorringe, Petra Gill, Doris Jewson, Ethel Mairet. By courtesy of Petra Tegetmeier

attitudes; most had neither studied nor worked before. When asked if she felt part of a pioneering craft, Petra Tegetmeier replied:

Well, yes, we were rather. After the War, all these people were feeling they wanted to do something rather than go back to the commercial world, rather like Valentine [KilBride], and there was a lot of unemployment then I suppose. I don't remember there being any weaving and there certainly wasn't the amount of spinning that there is done today – you can even buy spinning wheels in England, before you had to buy them in Sweden or somewhere.[9]

As well as the apprentices, a further group of regular work girls who lived locally were employed from the beginning of the twenties through to the outbreak of war in 1939; they were trained in the workshop to spin, make warps and throw the shuttle as directed. Ethel Mairet liked always to have four such "village girls" at any one time.

In practice, very little spinning was carried out on the premises, although one or two younger girls came in from the village for lessons. The hand-spun yarn normally used for the weft was supplied by the few woollen spinners who lived nearby or by the work girls who took fleece home to spin in the evenings, using Ethel Mairet's equipment. Ethel Mairet had evolved her own short-draw method of spinning, which she taught to the apprentices and work girls, who were supposed to be able to understand every stage of both the preparation of yarn and the weaving of cloth. Instruction was by example; very little formal teaching was given, and during the early years no use was made of Ethel Mairet's collection of foreign and historical textiles. As Doris Jewson, an apprentice in the early 1920s, commented, "We were just left to get on with it."[10]

The work produced at Gospels during the 1920s was characterised by rich, simple weavings and a concentration on dyeing. Ethel Mairet was making revisions for the third edition of her dyebook, published in 1924, and unwittingly the chief dye apprentices, Valentine KilBride and Petra Gill, were probably assisting in this. (KilBride certainly made trials for the Turkey Red item.) Many cold hours were spent in the dyehouse or the yard, but KilBride, already an expert chemical dyer trained in Bradford, and the sixteen-year-old Petra preferred the duties there (soaking, washing yarns or finishing the cloth) to the sometimes tempestuous climate in the weaving room. Although the dyebook contains innumerable recipes, the dyes most in use at Gospels were the imported indigo, madder and cochineal, and the British plants weld, bracken and crotal. These were capable of being treated by different mordants or of being overdyed with other colours, but most often the colours were used in their pure hues. Dyeing was a popular subject and from about 1926 Ethel Mairet taught short courses in the subject ("dye weeks"), the first events organised for outsiders to be held at Gospels. Margery Kendon, a student at the time and later an apprentice, has given an account of the one she attended in 1926:

She charged about two guineas and everybody enjoyed it; and she got a whole batch of wool dyed that the workshop could use throughout the winter. And then we used to go up on the Downs and collect weld. It was a wonderful week. She did not grow dye plants in the garden in my day; she did later on. Throughout the year there would be dye days every week unless it had to be put off for the weather. Of course, there was an underground tank, we always had soft water. There were galvanised baths on a long (8 foot long × 14 inches wide) wood and coal fire in a long channel; it would take five baths side by side with tin plates between and then the thing would turn round and go up the chimney, it had a wonderful draught. She was very particular about the way we lifted things; she wasn't going to have any strained muscles. We had to have our feet together, we lifted a bath with someone else and then we'd turn it up outside the dye shed on the concrete. Then we'd leave it to cool and pick out the skeins and shake them to get the madder out, or whatever it was. It was a real hard day's work. She

The weaving room at Gospels in the early 1920s. Inset: Valentine KilBride and Petra Gill in the dyehouse yard, c. 1923. Photographs from the Gospels Album, by courtesy of John Piper

would always put the madder in, she was better at dyeing madder than anyone else, and Elizabeth Peacock was better at dyeing cochineal than anyone else; I loved madder.[11]

The yarns in use were primarily wool, with silk and cotton introduced in great quantity after 1924. Fleece was obtained from the firm of Ebenezer Prior, woolstaplers of Chichester, from whom Ethel Mairet and the apprentices learnt a great deal on their visits to the premises. All her life Ethel Mairet was interested in the study of sheep and the various types of fleece; she experimented with many breeds but the one she most commonly used was Southdown. She sought yarn from any animal source and once asked the apprentices to try and spin the hair from one of her dogs (she kept Samoyeds at first, then Alsatians) but the experiment was a failure. For the warp she chiefly used machine-spun undyed woollen yarns, which were bought in from and named after individuals who had, by coincidence, been apprenticed to the workshop in its formative years. They included the

Ethel and Philip Mairet (right) with a visitor outside Gospels, 1923–4
Opposite: During her time in India and Ceylon Ethel Mairet amassed a very fine collection of woven and embroidered textiles, now housed at the Crafts Study Centre in Bath

Samples of hand-spun and vegetable-dyed eri silk from the early years at Gospels; plain weave, some with crammed weft stripes; Gospels Workshop, 1920–33. Crafts Study Centre, Bath

Inset Knee rug in hand-spun, undyed and vegetable-dyed wool; plain weave with crammed weft stripes, blanket-stitched ends; 192 cm × 78 cm; Gospels Workshop, 1920–25. Crafts Study Centre, Bath

This page Background: tablecloth of
hand-spun, vegetable-dyed cotton;
plain weave with occasional crammed
weft stripes, fringed ends;
160 cm × 73 cm; Gospels Workshop,
c. 1925. On top: stole of hand-spun,
vegetable-dyed and undyed eri silk;
plain weave with crammed weft stripes
and inlaid border pattern, fringed
ends; 198 cm × 73 cm; Gospels
Workshop, probably woven by
Elizabeth Peacock, c. 1920. Crafts
Study Centre, Bath

Opposite page: see overleaf

Background: dress or jacket fabric in machine-spun, undyed Welsh wool weft on a machine-spun, undyed fine cotton warp; plain weave, spaced reeding; 279 cm × 72 cm; Gospels Workshop, 1938–40. On top: sleeve of jacket in undyed thick wool and dyed fine cotton weft on an undyed fine cotton warp; all yarns machine-spun; plain weave, spaced reeding; length at centre back 56 cm; Gospels Workshop, 1939, made for Edith Solomon. Also shown: samples and a swatch of Ethel Mairet's dress fabrics; wool and silk doublecloths and textured four- and eight-shaft weaves in various combinations of yarns; weaves introduced by Marianne Straub; Gospels Workshop, 1933–4. Crafts Study Centre, Bath

Previous page Background: tablecloth woven by Ethel Mairet, using her characteristic madder dye; hand-spun, vegetable-dyed and undyed eri silk weft on a machine-spun, undyed cotton warp; distorted weft effect; 91.5 cm × 86.5 cm; Gospels Workshop, 1928–32. Jacket: also woven by Ethel Mairet; hand-spun, vegetable-dyed and undyed eri silk; plain weave in non-repeating stripes, some using colour-and-weave effect; bound edges, turned wooden buttons by Fred Partridge; length 61 cm; Gospels Workshop, 1925–30. Crafts Study Centre, Bath

from MRS. MAIRET
GOSPELS, DITCHLING, SUSSEX

Examples of experimental wefts introduced at Gospels. Background: scarf in hand- and machine-spun, dyed wool weft on a machine-spun, dyed cotton warp; plain weave, spaced reeding, extra weft stripes with cut floats; 88 cm × 24 cm; Gospels Workshop, 1938–45. Folded scarf: machine-spun, undyed wool and single tussah silk weft on a machine-spun, dyed cotton warp; plain weave, spaced reeding; 94 cm × 21 cm; Gospels Workshop, 1933–5. Samples: machine-spun, dyed wool in plain weave with raised loops or intermittent threads of hand-spun, undyed wool in the wefts; Gospels Workshop, 1935–7. Crafts Study Centre, Bath

The yellow-and-black check fabrics for which Ethel Mairet was known in the later years. Background: dress fabric in machine-spun, dyed and undyed Welsh wool weft on a warp of the same yarn plus machine-spun, dyed cotton; plain weave; 402 cm × 70 cm; Gospels Workshop, 1940–50. Scarf: machine-spun, dyed cotton slub and undyed chenille weft on a machine-spun, dyed cotton warp; plain weave, spaced reeding, fringed ends; 114 cm × 18 cm; Gospels Workshop, 1944–50. Crafts Study Centre, Bath

Furnishings from the 1940s at
Gospels, experimenting with
materials. Rug (*above*): braided
parachute cord and machine-spun,
dyed wool weft on a bast fibre warp;
plain weave with weft stripes and
inlaid design, fringed ends; 157 cm × 74 cm;
Gospels Workshop, 1943–4. Crafts
Study Centre, Bath

Cushion cover: machine-spun, dyed fancy cotton and uncoloured cellophane strip weft on a machine-spun, undyed cotton warp; plain weave; 39.5 cm × 34 cm; Gospels Workshop, 1940–50. Wallhanging: machine-spun, undyed linen, cotton and sisal, and uncoloured cellophane weft on a machine-spun, undyed cotton warp; plain weave, spaced reeding, fringed ends; 203 cm × 104 cm; Gospels Workshop, 1940–46. Crafts Study Centre, Bath

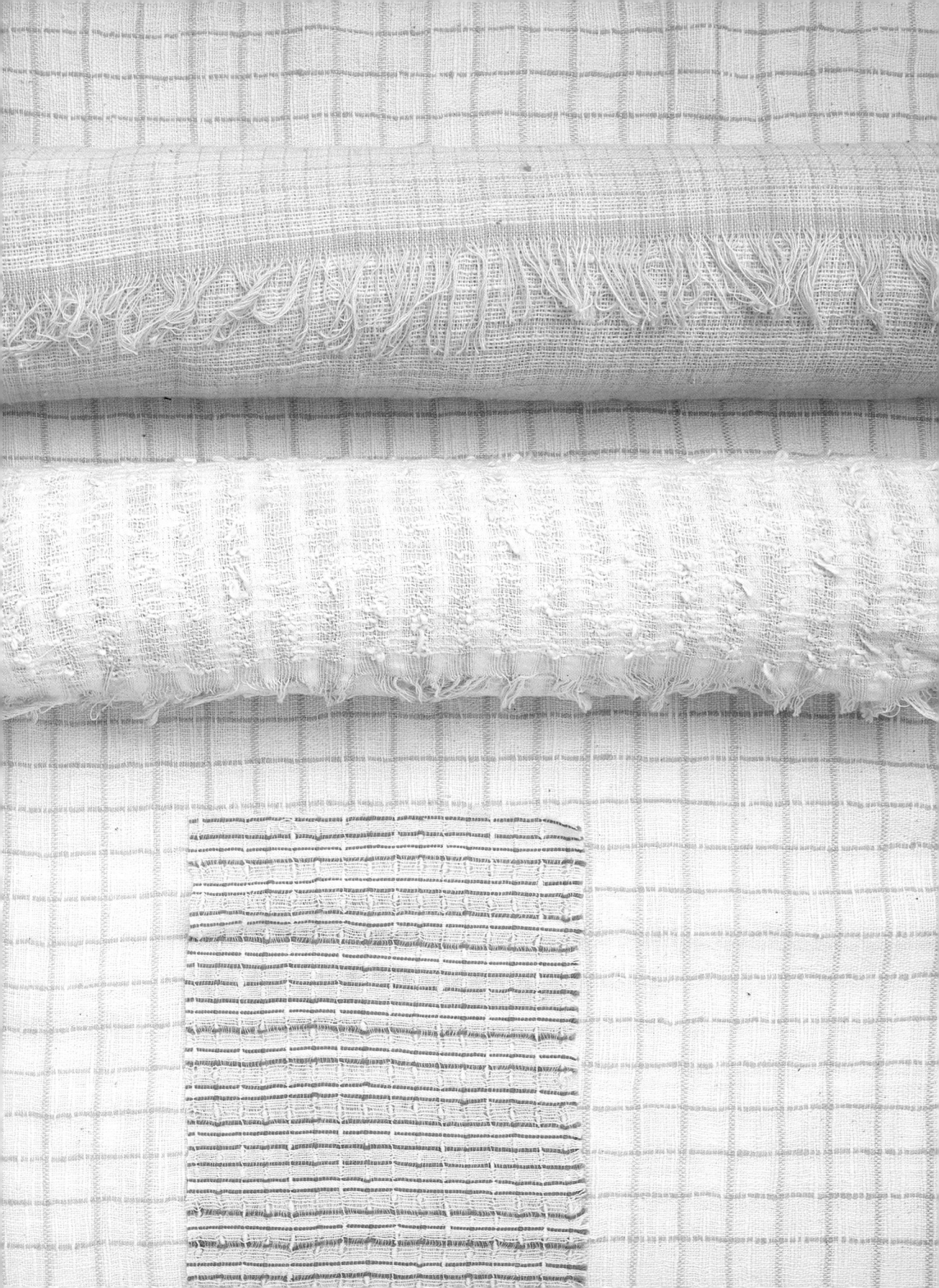

Previous pages, left Background: blouse fabric in undyed cotton slub and tussah silk weft on a dyed and undyed cotton warp; machine-spun yarns; plain weave forming a check; 426 cm × 71 cm; Gospels Workshop, 1938–45. Top roll of blouse fabric: dyed and undyed, machine-spun cotton; plain weave forming a check; 385 cm × 74 cm; Gospels Workshop, 1938–45. Lower roll: undyed, looped cotton spiral and undyed, fine man-made fibre weft on an undyed cotton warp; machine-spun yarns; plain weave, spaced reeding; 283.5 cm × 68.5 cm; Gospels Workshop, 1944–52. Sample (*below*): undyed cotton knop and fine man-made fibre weft on a striped cotton warp; machine-spun yarns; plain weave, spaced reeding; 18 cm × 35 cm; Gospels Workshop, 1944–5. Crafts Study Centre, Bath

Previous pages, right Open-textured weavings from the last years at Gospels. Stole (*left*): undyed chenille, undyed continuous filament rayon and machine-spun, dyed cotton slub weft on a dyed and undyed, machine-spun cotton warp; plain weave, spaced reeding, cut weft loops, fringed ends; 213.5 cm × 45.5 cm; Gospels Workshop, 1948–52. Scarf (*right*): machine-spun, dyed cotton gimp and hand-spun, undyed wool weft on a machine-spun, dyed and undyed cotton warp; plain weave, spaced reeding, fringed ends; 108 cm × 20 cm; Gospels Workshop, 1948–52. Crafts Study Centre, Bath

Above From the mid 1930s at Gospels, there was greater awareness of garment design and fabric was often ordered to be made up into tailored clothes. Jacket: machine-spun, dyed wool, undyed silk and hand-spun, madder-dyed Southdown wool weft on a machine-spun, dyed wool warp; plain

weave ground with thick weft floats; carved mahogany buttons by Fred Partridge; length 60 cm; Gospels Workshop, 1939, made for Edith Solomon; cloth designed by Marianne Straub c. 1934. Victoria & Albert Museum

Right An example of Ethel Mairet's earliest weavings at her workshop in Shottery. Pinafore dress; hand-spun, vegetable-dyed wool; alternating threads of brown and ochre in the warp, blue weft; twill weave; trimmed with hand-woven wool braid and wool embroidery; belt clasp of brass wire and embroidery, maker unknown; length from shoulder to hem 124 cm; matching cap, not shown; Shottery, Stratford on Avon, c. 1916, made for Estella Canziani. Museum of London

Baker Warp, a two-ply yarn used from about 1922 and sold by Denis Baker from his Stratford workshop, and the KilBride Warp, used continuously from about 1925 to 1933; the latter was a primitively machine-spun yarn obtained in the Pyrenees by the engraver Philip Haygreen and sent to KilBride, who was then working on Ditchling Common. The supply probably failed when KilBride gave up weaving tweeds and turned entirely to silk vestment cloth, but it is possible that there were large stocks of such yarns at Gospels even when they had been superseded by others; similarly Ethel Mairet might still have been using up Shottery stock, probably Shetland yarn, for a long period. The introduction of Assam or eri silk and both native-spun and raw cotton can be attributed to the British Empire Exhibition of 1924–5 at Wembley which was designed to illustrate the ways in which British firms used raw materials from the Empire; at the close of the exhibition Mairet and Peacock bought large amounts of the various fibres, and the effect of these is seen in their work. Through this exhibition Ethel Mairet was able to secure further supplies of the heavy lustrous silk yarn which she so loved and which responded so well to strong natural dyes.

The character and style of Gospels weavings were influenced immeasurably by those who passed through the workshop and by Ethel Mairet's ability to grasp an opportunity when it presented itself. Contemporary with Denis Baker in 1921 and 1922 were two cousins from Haslemere, Hilda Woods and Ursula Hutchinson; both middle-aged, they came with the desire to run a workshop of their own. At Ditchling the cousins lived in a gipsy caravan. Ursula Hutchinson's diary reveals (apart from her adulation of Ethel Mairet) that she wove hatbands (or braids), scarves and skirt lengths. The braids were an early and short-lived form probably designed as a decorative binding to the raw edges on the currently fashionable "djibbahs [jumpers] and jerkins", loose T-shaped garments of plain woollen cloth favoured at Gospels which the Inval Weavers, and many weavers since, appear to have imitated. In exchange Hutchinson and Woods contributed to the workshop by introducing looms made by Dolloway, the cabinetmaker who had previously supplied the Haslemere Weaving Industry; several pieces of equipment were acquired from this source. Dolloway later moved his business to Petts Wood, Kent.

The equipment *in situ* when Ethel Mairet set up her workshop was indeed basic; half a dozen or so second-hand looms from Shottery, including a braid loom on which Maud Partridge often worked. It improved marginally a few years later when the looms from Haslemere were added, and again in the thirties when two Danish eight-shaft Lervad looms were added. (Up to this time, all the looms had been four-shaft and from the UK.) Ethel Mairet was from the start uninterested in, and even hostile to, textiles which relied for their effect on the clever manipulation of gadgetry. For the first decade at Ditchling she used only plain weave. She was extremely fortunate that Valentine KilBride joined the workshop in its first phase. He had a great deal of technical experience, and had had hand-looms built to Luther Hooper's design under his charge; he would very often mend and untangle equipment for the work girls and apprentices. Although Ethel Mairet admired and trusted him as a dyer and technician, he did not stand out as a designer in her mind. Petra Tegetmeier recalls:

Mrs M tended to find his work rather dull because he had worked in the big mills in Bradford and he was a perfectionist and couldn't bear this sort of knobbly thing that we rather liked, the hand-spinning must be absolutely perfect. The weaving was beautiful but he tended to make it look like machine-weaving. I always remember this, because it was a thing that I could never have done: he had a special little gadget that would make the exact number of rows to the inch – a little measure. I've never seen one before or since but that was his method of weaving; he felt that you ought to have the right weight cloth, the warp and the weft should be absolutely perfect. Whereas we used to spin our wool and weave it and she used to like that sort of "hand look" about it.[12]

Here we have the contrasting approaches of the highly trained industrial producer, unwilling to accept unconventional methods and results, and the intuitive craftsman who feels untold technical prowess would be a barrier to artistic human creativity. The conflict between humanism and technology was to be a problem in the development of Ethel Mairet's ideas and work. For many years, continuing into the 1930s, she cherished late nineteenth-century Arts and Crafts Movement ideas of re-creating a pre-industrial society (of which the workshop was a microcosm), whose products would be fashioned entirely by hand, whose makers not only made their own clothes but baked their own bread, made their own music and were of high moral fibre. It was as if the Jazz Age had never existed.

The weavings themselves were of a very simple nature, used as scarves, shawls or stoles, cushions, knee rugs and, early on, small floor rugs. These were in wool or silk and were items from the moment they came off the loom, involving no further processes. They were conceived as rectangles or strips, relying on the contrasts and harmonies of clear colour arranged as "all-over stripes" or patterned borders, worked on four shafts, or some large and primitive inlay motif. A ready market existed for the smaller items and Ethel Mairet took part in the numerous selling exhibitions of the period and sold through private galleries (see page 107 ff). In addition she produced short lengths of loosely woven plain-coloured wool tweed and silk (the latter takes dye particularly well because of the refractory surface of the fibres) for making up into djibbahs, jackets and skirts, although there is no record of a regular dressmaker being employed at Gospels between 1920 and 1930. Samples of a heavy natural-coloured cotton cloth, suitable for furnishing, and the mention of an unusual shiny material being woven into a tablemat were breaks with tradition, and evidence of experimentation in the workshop.

The overall effect, however, was of richly coloured cloths to wrap oneself in or to adorn a favourite oak settle; it was what today we should call "ethnic" and as such it was highly regarded among the cognescente and seen as faintly unclean by the rest. It would be hard to claim that textiles of this type were actually designed; they were never drawn up as colour ideas or as threading drafts (these were beyond Ethel Mairet). Margery Kendon explains:

You got your inspiration from the loom; we never thought of it but she used to get furious with people who had had an art school training and who would work it out on paper first. She couldn't stand that, that was wicked. You did what the spirit moved you to do. Nobody ever said "That won't stand up as a skirt" because it did stand up – by willpower![13]

Ethel Mairet's approach to weaving was that it should be an intuitive and expressive response to the colour and texture of the yarn, for its own sake and not for the patterns it could be made into – she was infatuated by yarn. It was a purely abstract concept, and because of its essentially direct nature it found ready adherents among the apprentices, who subsequently followed it in their own workshops. In the wrong hands, this approach to weaving became an empty, uncritical arty-craftiness which revelled in ill-chosen colours and mediocre yarns, but Ethel Mairet avoided this by her instinctive appreciation of colour. In his journals, Ashbee described the scene at Ditchling in November 1923:

Ethel Mairet and her brother Fred Partridge and her husband PAM (now an actor at the Old Vic after an unsuccessful venture into stained glass and concrete building), and George Chettle and many others make together a very fine and happy colony with a lot of the old Campden and Essex House spirit in it. Ethel in the centre of it all with her wonderful weaving shops, her looms and carpets and dyed stuffs. She has the soul of Oriental colour in her.[14]

CHAPTER 8
EUROPEAN TRAVELS
1927 - 1938

For as long as funds were available, and even when they weren't and she had to sell the piano or to borrow, Ethel Mairet never lost the habit of travel. Whether it was her weekly visits to London on business, annual trips to Manchester for the Red Rose Guild Exhibition, a holiday at Broadlys or more ambitious schemes to Europe, external stimulus was vital. As her work grew more widely known, she became occupied with more commitments away from Gospels and her actual practice of weaving and dyeing was reduced to a few hours a day. One of the chief diversions (to be discussed below) was the formation of the New Handworkers' Gallery with her husband Philip in 1927. During its planning the Mairets went on a tour of Yugoslavia, stopping *en route* to explore Paris and Trieste.

Ethel Mairet's journeys usually had a purpose: in Ceylon she had collected examples for study and the writing of *Mediaeval Sinhalese Art* (whilst incidentally furnishing the Norman Chapel), and in India for the exhibition with which Coomaraswámy was involved. Her interest at the time centred on embroidery: dark blue cotton betel bags and pillow covers from Kandy, hangings and carpets from Bokhara, lengths of sari cloth and embroidered silk garments. The collection also includes many other textiles: Kashmir shawls, flat-weave hand-spun tree cotton mats with geometric or bird designs, a saddle bag, braids and other treasures. The night before she sailed from Bombay for the last time she recorded the purchase of a Shikapuri yellow satin skirt, an embroidered Kashmir coat and a piece of red silk.

On all her journeys Ethel Mairet noted everything of interest in her journals, of which twelve have survived. On the trip to Yugoslavia she shows equal enthusiasm for sailing boats, porpoises, buildings, trees in fruit, people and every stitch they wear, household items for sale in the markets and Macedonian embroidery.

The first Yugoslav she discussed embroidery with was Lugo Kraja, with whom she immediately formed a friendship when she visited his shop. The greater part of the two journals recording her visits to Yugoslavia (the first with Philip, the second alone) is taken up with descriptions of the shops and markets where she went to look at textiles and yarns, and to see what the country people were wearing. This was what Ethel Mairet was interested in – the indigenous crafts, the hand-spun yarns and traditional fabrics of the older people's clothes. On her first visit she bought shoes, socks and belts (all of woven cloth), books, flax, a pony's nose bag and a striped potato sack. The first sack she saw was in use and the owner refused to sell, but she pursued the matter and bought one in a market, and was eventually taken to see the fabric being spun and woven deep in the country. The potato sack did duty in the workshop as a model of design, as Margery Kendon remembers: "I remember when she brought these things back . . . I did a skirt definitely inspired by a potato sack which was hand-spun, hand-woven goat's hair from Dalmatia, beautiful; you got things like that as inspiration."[1] Ethel Mairet even tried to buy things off people's backs; walking up a mountain they met "a delightful man of the best peasant type, carried a splendid shawl of dark brown cloth with small pattern border at the ends, tried to buy it but he wouldn't sell."[2]

On the first Yugoslav trip Philip kept the "accounts" meticulously, from the cab to Plumpton down to the cherries bought in München on their return. In 1930 Ethel Mairet returned alone, this time not only looking for ideas and inspiration but also as a collector of things to sell. She did not specify where they would be sold, but at this date it could have been the New Handworkers' Gallery or Gospels. As soon as she arrived, on 8 May, she "spent most of the morning with Lugo Kraja looking at his things".[3] Later she records "getting shoes with Draga"[4] and Draga became a regular contact for the import of brightly patterned knitted socks and slippers to supply the shop Ethel Mairet ran in Brighton between 1935 and 1945 (see pages 112–14). The total amount of small items (bags, belts, braids, shoes, socks, aprons, boxes etc.), lengths of cloth, rugs and mats purchased in May and June 1930 came to 29,000 dinars which, using the conversion rate noted by Philip for the previous trip, was about £120 sterling. The stuff was parcelled up and sent home by post.

She consistently sought out plain hand-spun wools and cottons while constantly commenting on the varying quality of colours and the lack of natural dyes. Although Yugoslavia was no longer a primitive society, hand-weaving had not died out and some of her hosts shared her concern for its survival. Among them was Miss Dickinson, who collected locally woven aprons and linen dresses; she ran a small woodwork business in Travnik which produced simple brightly stained furniture for which the aprons were made into cushions. She took Ethel Mairet to see a peasant weaver up in the hills; the account is one of the most interesting in the journals:

Went in the afternoon three miles up in the hills to see a weaver and embroiderer. A peasant cottage on the side of the hill, very clean, with a nice little garden, on hand a cow, chickens.

One large room, no furniture except two or three stools, a stove, two small looms; leading out was a small sort of a kitchen scullery with an open fire on a raised brick hearth, burning wood, outside a cowshed and loft. Woman, husband died, and she carries it all on, three children. Weaves all her own things, bed-mattress covers (coarse hemp warp and rag weft), blankets in striped natural black and white coarse wool, cotton dresses for the children and herself, coloured cotton head wraps, blue-coloured waistcoats. She spins her own wool and hemp, but the linen they do very seldom as the seed costs a lot and they can't afford it. Only the richer families can afford seed.

She also makes a plaited red braid about $1\frac{1}{2}$ inches wide with 12 threads. They use it for bridles, apron strings, etc. It is tied on the end of a sort of spindle distaff which she stuck in her belt. The looms are small, about 22 inches wide, and she had on a white cotton warp which she crossed with red cotton striped with dark blue – completely covering the warp. The other loom was with a striped hand-spun wool for men's belts. She buys her cotton in a shop in Travnik, Italian cotton, and dyes it herself in the kitchen. She was dyeing a dark red but it is all chemical dyes. She brings her surplus cotton stuff in to a shop in Travnik which sells them for her.[5]

The weavings Ethel Mairet admired most in Yugoslavia were the aesthetic parallels of her own work but in country families weaving was done out of necessity. In Scandinavia, which she visited in 1932, 1933, 1936 and 1938, the situation was different but equally enviable. Hand-weaving had a place in modern life and design, strongly related to architecture; weavers were a small but well-respected body of craftsmen. She visited three schools of weaving in Denmark and became associated with the Askov Weaving School, run by Miss Trock and Miss Baumann, where, briefly, she taught spinning. The Askov school was recognised by the state education author-ities and some of the students were grant-aided; it was well equipped with looms for all kinds of work, including carpet weaving. Although Ethel Mairet chose to ignore the strongly patterned nature of the work at Askov,

Ethel Mairet's visits abroad are well documented; a list of purchases, a receipt and her journal for May 1930, with a pair of the socks she later imported and sold at her shop in Brighton

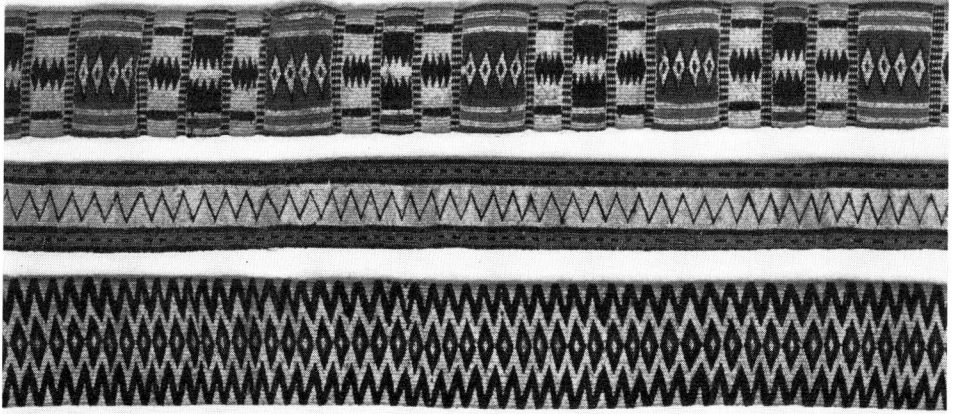

Samples of Yugoslavian woven braids and belts, made of wool and goats' hair

Ethel Mairet (centre) with Miss Trock and Miss Baumann at Askov in Denmark, June 1933

and in Denmark generally, she was increasingly drawn to linen weaving and to linen embroidery. Miss Trock and Miss Baumann introduced her to a weaver friend of theirs named Baroness Wedell, who worked with Astrid Jacobson; at their studio she was shown furnishings and particularly commented on some open-weave linen curtaining with wool inlay, which was pronounced "good taste".

The purpose of her first trip to Denmark in September 1932 was to attend an exhibition of textiles at the Kunst Industrie Museum in Copenhagen, in which she had been asked to participate by the British Council. Her presence was obviously of some note for she gave a lecture, was interviewed by the Press (over tea) and was generally courted by museum directors and eminent people who entertained her and took her sightseeing. A favourite excursion was to the Folk Museum where she saw the typical intricate patterns of fine woven linen inlaid with wool, used traditionally for dresses. On her visit in June the following year, accompanied by apprentice and associate Margery Kendon, Ethel Mairet returned to Askov where she showed a marked interest in Danish looms. She bought an eight-shaft loom from the loom-maker Lervad, although she had no idea how to use it, and also noted the cheaper Clausen looms. Margery Kendon stayed on to teach and study at the Askov Weaving School.

For all her compatability with Denmark, Ethel Mairet found Finland, and Helsinki in particular, her spiritual home. In her journal she enthuses about all she saw: the granite and concrete station building designed by Saarinen, the restaurants and, most of all, Stockmans, "a fine modern shop for every-thing – interesting things in all the departments"[6]; she returned there many times, and it was there that she found and bought her little red spinning wheel as well as, no doubt, various textiles. The journey continued via Estonia on the Baltic coast, where she bought tweeds for her collection, then on to Stockholm where she encountered the thoroughly modernistic work of Elsa Gullberg; she thought it fine and "ranking with Rodier * in quality"[7] Elsa Gullberg was the first weaver-designer, producing hand-woven prototypes for industry, that Ethel Mairet had ever met; immediately she recognised this as the way forward, the way ahead to better textiles generally. From now on she stopped looking exclusively to hand-spun pea-sant textiles and turned instead to thinking of Elsa Gullberg's mode of operation: "She makes the factories do the thread she wants for her textiles and dictates colour and works with them. They help her by producing in quantity the kind of materials she wants not too expensively."[7] The tex-tiles which most impressed her were "quite cheap linen tablecloth stuff" with large areas of plain colour on a white and grey pattern and "beautiful plain simple warp-striped cotton".[7]

Ethel Mairet returned with a large number of items for her collection and probably with some for re-sale: belts, braids and lace, wooden spoons, bowls and trays, tablet weavings, a purse, a shuttle, many pairs of gloves, mats, bags and four Faröe Island sweaters. She particularly liked the soft, thick Faröe wool, samples were requested, and very soon it appeared both as a warp and weft at Gospels. Kate Drummond, who visited Gospels in the mid-thirties, emphasised the strong influence of this trip on her work: "She was the first British weaver to go to Finland and Scandinavia and she came back with examples of their weaving and filled with enthusiasm."[8]

In June 1936 Ethel Mairet made another short trip to Finland, where for the first time she records seeing rag rugs and also notes a novel way of cutting striped linen for making cushion covers. She made several visits to Stockmans and talked to the weaver in charge of the crafts department, Mrs Sittnikow, and noted all the names of the weavers exhibited in the shop: Greta Skogster Lechtinen, Marta Taipale, Eva Antilla, Dora Jung, Brita Mether, Toni Kallio. The work of Greta Skogster attracted her comments for its strong sense of material and texture; she noted "bands of warp without weft" and bought a piece for her collection. The previous day she

---

*Rodier was a French designer of hand-woven fabrics, used for couture clothes, which exploited the possibilities of technique and fibre.

had met and talked with the architect and maker of furniture Alvar Aalto: ''a very real person, the best type of craftsman'',[9] the embodiment of Ashbee's ''standard'' in a modern age.

In the intervening years at Gospels several European girls, usually trained weavers, had passed through the workshop and left their mark on its products. Ethel Mairet had most rapport with Marianne Straub, a Swiss designer by then working in England; they visited Finland together in 1936, and in 1938 they travelled through Europe in search of weaving, at the same time looking up old friends and acquaintances. They sailed from Hull, stopping at Copenhagen and Helsinki, where they made a visit to the spinning factory at Ekenäs, the first time Ethel Mairet had seen machine spinning in operation. The small hand-controlled mule made it possible to spin limited quantities of each colour, thus increasing the range the factory was able to stock, something which greatly impressed Ethel Mairet. They flew to Viipuri and then went on by train to Lake Lagoda where they visited the workshop of Greta Skogster, one of the best-known weavers of furnishing fabrics in Finland. She was away at the time but they saw round the workshop which

(Left to right) Ethel Mairet, Mrs Boije, Miss Brueneck and Marianne Straub at Ekenas in Finland, 1938

Ethel Mairet shopping in Helsinki market in 1936

contained about twenty jacquard and shaft hand-looms; it was much more sophisticated than any workshop Ethel Mairet had ever seen.

The journey continued to Estonia and then on to Berlin, where an international crafts exhibition was the main attraction. Compared to the other European exhibitors, the British stand looked very poor:

It was the worst set of exhibits. . . . Too much silver, printed stuffs impossible. Dull old-fashioned gloves. The whole gave the impression of dullness and old-fashioned beside the brilliant displays of the other countries. They want to see our typical good work of today – the best tweeds, our splendid ironwork, in both of which we are better than anyone.[10]

Ethel Mairet spoke German so from her next visit, to the Textil und Modefachschule, she was able to glean a great deal of the background philosophy and teaching methods. The weaving teachers, for instance, gave three days teaching per week and spent the other three working days producing things in their own workshops. She writes enthusiastically about the fashion and dress department but observes that, "No class is just on its own – but all classes connect with each other."[11] Further stimulation came from the numerous arts and crafts shops in the city and from the Deutsches Heimatwerk (the equivalent of the Rural Industries Bureau) where she bought rag rugs for her collection.

Whilst in Berlin Ethel Mairet found several new types of yarn for her workshop. Over tea with a group of former helpers at Gospels (Dora Schiemann, the hostess, Maria Holstein, Helene Sinks and Grete Hinze) she was shown a piece of cellophane material by a Fraulein Fichard, but this she did not like because, being made partly of rayon, it looked "like gold brocade too much". She also visited the Bauhaus-trained weaver Margaret Leischner (she later came to England and taught at the Royal College of Art) who, among other things, showed her experiments using black cellophane and black synthetic horsehair together. Whilst acknowledging Leischner's enthusiasm and individuality, Ethel Mairet found her inartistic and rather hard, a trait she attributed to her nationality, although she did not come away without the address of the cellophane supplier. Before leaving Berlin she made another trip to the exhibition and at the Greek section ordered a kilo of unspun silk, some cotton yarn and a spindle. The spinner, from Athens, demonstrated the use of left to right spindle-spun yarn for the warp and right to left for the weft; the resulting cloth "hung marvellously".

Marianne Straub took Ethel Mairet to stay with her family in Switzerland, and introduced her to Heinz Otto Hürlimann and Gunta Sharon Stölzl, two notable weavers from the Bauhaus. Hürlimann showed her round the weaving department of the Kunstgewerbeschule where he taught and which Marianne Straub and Bianca Wassmuth (an assistant at Gospels in 1933) had attended. The brevity of Ethel Mairet's journal entry suggests that she was not very impressed with the place, but she showed a growing interest in the gauze and leno techniques above the other weaving methods (jacquard and dobby) seen in the school. Following this visit, they went to the studio of Frau Sharon Stölzl, where she recorded: ''Small working studio, four or five looms, two women working. Jacquard – very good, interesting materials and colours.''[12] Ethel Mairet showed genuine approval for Hürlimann's use of cellophane yarn for cinema curtains and not long afterwards tried to use the material herself.

The Swiss connection proved useful in other ways. She had a meeting with Dr Laur of the Swiss Heimatwerk, through whom she learnt more about the organisation's workings and its support of the crafts in rural areas. It was a scheme which included assistance with the supply of materials to craftsmen and with the marketing of the final products. Ethel Mairet found this useful as a comparison with the Rural Industries Bureau in England and Wales; she had already had some sway in 1934 by suggesting that Marianne Straub be appointed designer to the small Welsh woollen mills.

In 1937 Mairet herself visited a number of Welsh mills for the first time and saw the small, struggling weaving industry in operation. The tour of Wales was by car and, since Ethel Mairet could not drive, was organised by her friend Margaret Pilkington, Director of the Whitworth Art Gallery in Manchester and organiser of the Red Rose Guild Exhibitions. In the remoter parts the car had to be abandoned and the mills reached on foot. Her journal contains a description of Mr Morgan's mill in Wallis, south-west Wales:

Inside very dark – all water power – there was a devil and a hand-controlled mule taking up all one shed, large peg warping board where he could warp 100 yards, a large hand-turned spinning wheel which he uses for winding bobbins, he showed us how it spun. Three small looms for tweeds and one large fly shuttle for blankets and stair carpet. Stair carpet very interesting, he uses 4 ply for warp, 4 shillings a yard. Sells his things in Haverfordwest market, used to walk in, now goes by bus – $8\frac{1}{2}$ miles.[13]

Shortly afterwards Morgan's of Wallis supplied some woollen yarn for use at Gospels workshop.

CHAPTER 9
DEVELOPMENTS AT
GOSPELS
1933-1938

The weavings developed in the thirties at Gospels are the ones on which
Ethel Mairet's current reputation is founded, although for those who knew
and participated in the workshop from 1922 to 1932 nothing could replace
the unique and ebullient spirit of the products from that decade.

Events at the beginning of this period were traumatic. In November 1930
the Mairets' joint venture into business, the New Handworkers' Gallery,
had moved to a far superior location at 6 Fitzroy Square, where it was
advertised as being run by Ethel Mairet and Gwendoline Norsworthy. No
sooner was this new arrangement underway than it failed: Mrs Norsworthy
and Philip Mairet formed an attachment and the entire situation exploded.
Philip left Gospels to live with Mrs Norsworthy, he broke with Mitrinovic
(whose nursing bills he had recently been paying) and the gallery closed.
The stock was transferred to Gospels, where terror reigned; during the
recent stormy period Ethel Mairet's temper had been at its height and she
had allegedly emptied the contents of drawers out of upstairs windows on
Philip's departure. Fortunately there were no apprentices living in the
house at this point, although a group of four or five workgirls and one
apprentice came in daily.

Philip Mairet described the break as "the complete destruction of my
previous way of life, occupational and domestic . . . a crisis of almost
complete disintegration".[1] Ethel Mairet, who always kept personal matters
under the surface, did not comment publicly, but it is clear that her person-
ality underwent a marked change. At the age of 58 she suddenly found
herself to be alone, emotionally isolated, with her second marriage a failure.

During the thirties she began to show signs of impatience and intolerance, and those who knew her in the twenties have commented on the contrast to her earlier spirit of freedom and gaiety. Her cure for depression was always a new project and she threw herself into her work, partly through financial necessity but also as an outlet for her strong-willed and independent character.

Mary Hill, a neighbour in Ditchling, has described Ethel Mairet at this time:

I shall never forget the first impact Gospels and the workshop made on me, the beautiful rich piles of hand-weaving were almost unbelievable after machine-made and dull material in the shops at that time. The workshop was to be an inspiration to many. She was a great craftswoman, a pioneer and a strong and courageous character, but she was not always an easy person and many stood in awe of her for she had, as well as strong likes, strong dislikes too and could be quite devastating in her judgements. Dmitri Mitrinovic remarked once after an explosion of strong words that "she was at times like a burning haystack, so much good in her went to waste".

. . . Gathering wild flowers on the downs or watching her making bread in the kitchen, she would talk of her great interest in the new in Art. She was intensely serious about her craft and excluded those who were not; she disliked the amateur, the folksy, women who wanted to please just themselves on a hand-loom, and spared none of them, Her support went to the teacher, schoolchildren, the professional; her encouragement to those who experimented with new materials and those who, on the hand-loom, designed for the machine.[2]

The workshop at Gospels was based on the apprenticeship system, one in which the Master maintained an elevated position. Ethel Mairet's principles, however, did not altogether follow the example of C. R. Ashbee's Guild. To start with, of course, the Gospels workshop did not resemble his multi-craft ideal; nor did Ethel Mairet follow the humanising ideals of the Guild in the provision of cottages, allotments, a bathing lake and entertainments such as the Guild plays and beanfeasts. In fact the social welfare at Gospels was non-existent although Ethel Mairet never ignored the needs of homeless or troubled girls, who sometimes arrived unannounced on her doorstep, and she was very generous about giving her apprentices time off and pocket money to go to see exhibitions in London.

The most obvious difference between the Gospels workshop and the Guild of Handicraft was that the Guild was run democratically, almost to the last. All the members were aware of the financial situation and the commissions in hand, and they were involved in the making of policy decisions. But information about the income and expenditure of Gospels workshop was not the province of the apprentices and workers. Ethel Mairet was something of an autocrat, less interested in social experiment than Ashbee, less able to create positions of responsibility for others. Several associates shied away from the idea of taking on the management of the workshop under her, but later on she did allow the manageress of her shop in Brighton a free hand and she positively welcomed innovation at the looms while also, in the early twenties, encouraging Valentine KilBride to take the lead in the dyeshed. (His sex, as well as aptitude, may have had a little to do with this.) In short, Gospels was not conditioned by what Ethel Mairet had seen of the Guild of Handicraft, nor does it seem to have been modelled on other establishments for none were as ambitious in scale as her own. Other weavers, Peacock or KilBride for example, normally had a partner or an assistant and, irregularly, a trainee; the potters worked in a similar mode. There were a greater number of people at the sculptor Eric Gill's workshop but even here, in the thirties, there appeared to be a greater level of individual responsibility. Hilary Bourne, a weaver who was brought up in Ditchling, remembers: ". . . she kept very much to herself, she didn't mix with the village and nor did any of her workers. The only one who we knew very well was her sister Maud; she kept the Sundown Tearooms, we all loved her, but Mrs Mairet we were very much in awe of."[3]

In the thirties Ethel Mairet's personal involvement in the workshop decreased noticeably. The manner in which the workshop was staffed or filled was reflected directly in the style of weaving; this applied not only to the cloth but also to the clothes. For a period from 1930 to 1932 a gap occurred in the flow of apprentices; only Marjorie Denman (now Marjorie Kenney) was in residence plus the well-trained daily workgirls who wove the staple products. At this time Ethel Mairet was absorbed with the New Handworkers' Gallery and the break-up of her marriage, and she was abroad for six weeks in 1930 and two weeks in 1932.

Marjorie Denman worked on "ordinary little floor rugs",[4] woven on a big Scandinavian loom in the cold outer shed next to the dyehouse; they were usually striped, using a hemp warp covered by a hand-spun weft. Miss Gull, a staunch spinner and maker-up for the workshop for generations, spun the weft which, in the interests of economy, was often composed of left-over wools plyed together. As Marjorie Kenney remembers, the workgirls produced lengths of plain-coloured tweeds: "There were shelves in the weaving rooms which always had to be kept stocked with lengths of material, and then the rugs we used to hang all round the wall."[5] (In 1932 Gospels was Ethel Mairet's sole regular selling outlet; also on sale were pottery and baskets from Braunton in North Devon.) A particular

The weaving room at Gospels, photographed for Queen *magazine in 1932*
Inset: Ethel Mairet spinning at Gospels, c. 1933

commission about which Ethel Mairet was "very excited" was the weaving of indigo blue altar rail kneelers for the chapel of Chailey Heritage, a crafts school for the handicapped. The kneelers (now lost) represent one of the two recorded commissions carried out for specific buildings; the second, dated 1943, was cellophane wallcoverings and seagrass matting for the premises of the British Drama League in Fitzroy Square. Another weave to appear at this time was a distorted weft effect, achieved by a four-shaft draft, in which the lines formed by the weft wander rhythmically; it is known colloquially as "Ms and Os" or sometimes "almond eye".

Ethel Mairet had returned from Denmark full of enthusiasm for modern hand-loom weaving and design in Europe and openly disdainful of the situation in Britain. In winter 1933 she devised the notion of a National or Central School of Weaving (including hand block-printing and embroidery). She sent a proposal to James Morton, who ran the two firms Morton Sundour and Edinburgh Weavers, in which she suggested that such a school needed sponsorship, that it should be outside London but easily accessible, should have teachers from Europe and lectures on all subjects "by competent modern international artists, craftsmen and manufacturers".[6] She stated the struggle experienced by excellent and experimental weavers (Dennis Baker, Elizabeth Peacock and herself) to afford materials and obtain staff with which to carry out their ideas, and roundly condemned the amateurs. The paper was idealistic and dynamic but it met with a cool response from the leader of one of the better textile firms. He was not convinced of the idea's worth and differed with Ethel Mairet on the state of the British textile industry. As Nikolaus Pevsner stated, his firm had been one of those which "consciously transferred this unconscious tradition of exquisite weaving to the factory and carefully developed it there".[7]

Meanwhile in 1933 the workshop had been radically altered by an influx of foreign girls from Scandinavia, Switzerland and Germany. Most stayed a few months or a year and a few settled in England. (A total of 28 foreign girls is recorded.) Not everyone worked in the weaving room, there was housework and cooking to be done and Ethel Mairet's recipe book is peppered with unusual dishes from several countries. The first arrival was Bianca Wassmuth (now Bianca Fischer) who had been introduced to Ethel Mairet by Ragna Kjelsberg of the Swiss Heimatwerk. She began work at Gospels on the strength of the fact that she had been able to answer "Yes" to the question, "Can you tie up an eight-shaft countermarch loom?" (The Lervad had recently been delivered.) Marianne Straub, who had been a fellow student at the Kunstgewerbe Schule, was at the time a student at Bradford Technical College, concentrating on cloth construction and weav-

Dye day at Gospels in the early 1930s; Ethel Mairet (bending down) with her workgirls Elsie, Rose, Olive and Lillian

ing mechanism; she spent her Whitsun holiday at Gospels and returned in the summer for a nine-month stay. Under their joint influence, the character of the cloth in the workshop changed dramatically: Wassmuth introduced cloths with more textural interest, such as a silk weft float in a woollen dress fabric, and Straub experimented with spaced warps and open weaves, ambitious mixtures of yarns, float weaves and double cloths. A double cloth with loosely woven coloured silk on one side and hand-spun natural Southdown wool on the reverse was one of her main achievements at Gospels. "There was a revolution there, completely,"[8] commented Marjorie Kenney.

The innovations pleased Ethel Mairet. Hilary Bourne remarked: "She loved change; her main thing was always to be up with the modern things

MISS FLAVIN
MARGERY KENDON
HILDE BILLER
    KAREN JØRGENSEN
    MARIANNE STRAUB

ELSE BILLER . GRETE . HIL...

HELGA ROGSTAD   ASA ROMSON
AGNETA DYSSEL, ELIZABETH SHALER

HILDE BILLER

MISS WIKLUND (SWEDEN)
DORA SCHIEMANN (GERMANY)
MISS BLAKSTAD (NORWAY)
GRETA AINZE (GERMANY)

MARIANNE STRAUB.

GRETE
MISS BLAKSTAD.
MISS WIKLUND.
MARTA WIBELL. (SWEDEN)

HILDE.

*Pages from the Gospels Album in the mid 1930s, showing the number and variety of people
passing through Gospels. By courtesy of John Piper*

and so she took Marianne as a textile designer . . . her *own* ways practically
faded out.''[9] The new ideas and drafts soon took over from the plain-weave
fabrics, silk stoles and scarves; Ethel Mairet's stand at the Red Rose Guild in
autumn 1933 looked completely different.

There was, however, nothing Marianne Straub wanted to change less
than the yarns used at Gospels; these she loved, revelling in their unusually
high quality and the rich or subtle colours which could be obtained with

ISE. BERYL , NELLY

MARGERY KENDON

HELGA + MISS GULL.

YE SHED

GRACE

vegetable dyes. Records show that from 1931 to 1937 cotton and silk was being taken to Valentine KilBride for dyeing, and he was selling indigo and madder to Ethel Mairet, probably for dyeing wool. Marianne Straub describes her eager appreciation of the yarns available in the workshop:

I remember the first warp I made at Gospels with about seven different hand-spun yarns. They all tore their hair and said, "Oh well of course that's much too difficult, you'll have an awful job putting that on," because they didn't use a raddle, they put it through the reed and of course there was a great deal of friction. My first week at Gospels was very hard because I made this lovely warp but it was very difficult to put on and the girls in the workshop thought that here was someone who was really bringing trouble![10]

Of the many foreign names, a further two should be mentioned in connection with specific weaving innovations: Dora Schiemann (1936–7), whose loop technique was responsible for many sophisticated, loosely woven shawls and stoles, and Leonora Maas, who set up and wove the gauze (leno) furnishings and shawl fabrics in 1939–40. She also spent some time at Elizabeth Peacock's establishment, Weavers.

To confirm her claim that she was running an "experimental workshop",[11] in 1934–5 Ethel Mairet took on her first English art school graduate, Joyce Winter (now Joyce Griffiths) who was being "put through" Gospels as an apprentice by her aunt Grace Crowfoot, the textile archaeologist. Like all new recruits who had never worked at a loom before, she wondered at the lack of instruction and learnt all she could of cloth construction from Marianne Straub and Agnete Dysell (a Danish weaver) so that she could dissect the fragments which her aunt discovered. Joyce Winter stayed a year, during which time she brought a more pronounced sense of form to the weavings. She used a variety of thick cottons in her cushion covers and curtains, which employed large geometrical areas of varying textures such as raised looped bands of hand-spun cotton on a flat ground.

During this period, Ethel Mairet experimented with several new materials, some discovered abroad and others found in England; plied silk obtained in Switzerland, hand-spun Russian linen found in a London street market, and machine-spun cotton from Maygrove's, a shop in the West End of London. Joyce Griffiths recalls:

She was very interested in different materials like cellophane, she went through a cellophane stage and a lurex stage. We used a lot of cellophane, she came home with it and tried carding it – a whole boxful of it – and tried to make a thread, I don't think it worked. We also used it in strips.[12]

While she was at Gospels, Joyce Winter became engaged to Hugh Griffiths, a student of weaving at the Central School of Art in London. After leaving college he set up a yarns business for hand-weavers and embroiderers, based largely on the suppliers whose names Ethel Mairet had passed on to him. The business continued for some thirty years, with Joyce Griffiths weaving to illustrate the numerous yarns.

Ethel Mairet's continuing influence in the workshop was not in the weave of the cloth but in the choice of yarns and her insistence on quality.

Her active involvement diminished sharply during this time, partly because her ideas had begun to dry up and because she was ill from stress and overwork. In 1935 she had to call on Margery Kendon to come and take over both the management of Gospels and the stand at the important White-chapel Art Gallery exhibition run by the Guild of Weavers, Spinners and Dyers; Ethel Mairet did not attend the event.

Although various weavings have been discussed in the context of innovation and in relation to given names, everything left the workshop under the name Gospels; at that date there was no cult of personalities as we know it today in the worlds of craft and design.

In the mid thirties Ethel Mairet built a substantial new weaving room next to the dyehouse, replacing the wooden shed which had stood there previously. Broadlys had been sold in 1931 and she probably used the proceeds for the new building, erected with the idea of increased activity in mind.

By 1938, when the number of foreign apprentices was beginning to diminish, the products of the workshop were allowed to regain a little of their old simplicity; plain weave was again exploited in the form of brightly coloured Assam silk checks or tartans, devised by Ethel Mairet and made up into shirt tops to be sold in her Brighton shop. These and loosely woven cottons dominated production during the war years. The workshop's supply of cotton had, since late 1938, come from R. Greg & Co., cotton spinners and doublers specialising in fancy yarns and at the time one of the most adventurous producers in the world.

Through the contact with Greg's, both plain and fancy cotton yarns played an increasingly important role in the production at Gospels. The plain yarns were used for spaced warp fabrics, "tartans" and "cotton tweeds", in which the cotton was crossed with wools of various weights. The fancy threads were used for the weft of more experimental fabrics, destined to be made up into blouses and jackets, or for furnishing. Colour was a less essential ingredient in the fabrics made with fancy yarns, partly because Ethel Mairet did little cotton dyeing herself; she used undyed yarn, plyed it with other yarns, or used the commercially dyed colours purchased from Greg or Maygrove.

Greg's dealt not only with cotton but with wool, flax and jute, and also man-made fibres such as rayon, fibro* and nylon. Stopford Jacks, then sales director of the firm, met Ethel Mairet at the Red Rose Guild exhibition, probably in 1938, and very soon afterwards Ethel Mairet spent a whole day

---

*A cut rayon staple fibre.

at Greg's mill in Stockport. The visit was reciprocated and in December 1938 Ethel Mairet wrote to Marianne Straub (then working as a designer for Helios in Bolton):

Several things have happened, the most important perhaps was that Mr Jacks came here to talk over yarns (of Greg & Co.), a very nice man, and the result was that he wants me to weave up samples with his yarns that he can have them to show customers – a very sound plan I think and it will be extremely interesting to do. I have chosen out a few I liked and shall go ahead directly he sends them. I want to try dyeing some as his colours are bad, but that will come later. Some of his yarns are so lovely that I want them for my work too. I can't see them yet as stuff but I am longing to get at them to see what they will do.[13]

Stopford Jacks spent half a day at Ditchling with Ethel Mairet "and very soon realised she was not a weaver, not a designer, but a yarn enthusiast – not just in the look of a yarn but also in the feel."[14] He had met this natural instinct for yarns in only a few other designers, notably Marianne Straub and Alistair Morton, but Ethel Mairet lacked their understanding of the mechanics of weaving and the problems of production. She showed him samples of fabrics from abroad using rough hand-spun yarns and asked if Greg's would produce special fancy yarns resembling them but, in the opinion of Mr Jacks, they were not commercially viable or possible. However they did find a way in which to work together, as Stopford Jacks explains:

The sequence of events was that my experience with Mrs Mairet convinced me that fancy yarns would be more acceptable to the fabric manufacturer if they could be shown to him in fabric form, the fabric being designed by a qualified weaver who had proved they were a commercial proposition on a mechanical loom. At that stage the War intervened and R. Greg & Co., had to concentrate on War work and there was little contact with Mrs Mairet. After the War I discussed the proposition with Alastair Morton [son of James Morton of Edinburgh Weavers] who was sympathetic and finally put me in touch with Margaret Leischner, trained at the Bauhaus. R. Greg & Co. employed her for some years designing fabrics with fancy yarns and provided her with hand-looms equipped with a dobby and a jacquard and other mechanical contrivances. Later the firm employed designers trained by Margaret at the Royal College of Art. My visits to Mrs Mairet continued: I found very stimulating her enthusiasm for the fancy effect. She always had something new to show me, and sometimes we were able to produce something by doubling and twisting – something which was also commercial. I think we helped her and certainly provided her with some yarns – but not being a weaver she never understood manufacturing or commercial problems. I think it was the feel of a yarn which interested her most.[15]

Ethel Mairet used many of Greg's fancy yarns, but of those which show her influence (nos. D870, 185 and 253) the only one which had commercial significance was the fine cotton snarl (185). This was produced largely at her instigation, she hand-dyed it and made it into scarves, and it was then put on the market and used by manufacturers of high-class furnishing fabrics. The production of this yarn was slow and difficult although it did become a standard small-order yarn. Her order books show that during the War she wove, and charged for, samples of cloth using various of Greg's fancy yarns. Ethel Mairet used to mount these fancy yarns on cards, together with examples of hand-spun yarns; looking at one of these recently, Stopford Jacks mused on the title she gave them: " 'An Adventure in Yarns' – it was!"

Stopford Jacks, every bit as direct as Ethel Mairet, has highlighted the areas of strength and weakness in her abilities, setting her in context with the designers who led the field in hand-woven design for industry in England from the late thirties. With the possible exception of Margaret Leischner, whose work Ethel Mairet regarded as cold, Alastair Morton and Marianne Straub were her favourite Modern Movement designers. Their influence helped her to come to terms with mechanical developments and synthetic fibres, which she expressed in her book *Hand-Weaving To-day* (1939) (see page 116).

The story of textiles, both "hand and machine", in the thirties is generally one of texture. Ethel Mairet herself arrived at this conclusion through her experiences in Europe, her contact with European designers at Gospels and her natural curiosity about yarns. But she should not be seen as the single pioneer in this field, she must be viewed in the context of a design movement which had recently become organised to form associations, government committees and the like to promote design and professionalism. Design had become respectable, serious and responsible; it showed a distinct preference for rationalism, functionalism and purity, inspired largely by the Modernist architects whose influence led to a greater interest in surface texture as part of design schemes, affecting textiles more than any other of the applied arts. Texture was obtained through the use of fancy yarns and broken-surfaced weaves; lighting became a tool with which to emphasise it.

A picture of the transitions which European textiles had undergone was given in *Textile Design* (1937) by Antony Hunt, himself a designer:

Probably the most remarkable feature of dress and furnishing fabrics during the past 25 years is their tremendous variety of texture. Never in the whole history of textiles have textures become so important, so numerous and, at times, so *outré*. . . .

Texture gradually became a dominant factor in fabric styles after the First World War when there was a thirst for innovation . . . and the younger architects, who were already exploring a variety of new surface treatments in building materials, welcomed and encouraged this texture-consciousness among interior decorators and their suppliers.

In France Rodier began to evolve his famous wool and goat's wool mixtures and Von Wecht, in Germany, his almost architecturally constructed hand-weaves. Edinburgh Weavers and Donald Brothers led the field in Britain. . . .

Textures obtained from fancy yarns having been extensively explored, broken surfaces in weaves themselves followed, to keep the insistence on textural interest alive.[16]

Another account of the times can be read in Nikolaus Pevsner's important report *Industrial Art in England*. He stresses the need for designers of woven textiles to understand the practical details of their craft and acknowledges the position of craftsmen who act as their own designers:

Commercially speaking, their workshops can hardly be taken as business enterprises at all. Quite often they are not paying propositions, and the artists live on "something of their own". Nevertheless the great experimental importance of such workshops is obvious, and they ought not to disappear, or at least they must have a refuge in art schools. For they alone keep up a direct unity between design and execution, and thus convey to the designer a live understanding of materials.[17]

The place Ethel Mairet held in all this was a small but singular one. She was acknowledged by the powers of "industrial art" (which during the thirties had metamorphosed into "design") and in 1938 she received the accolade of RDI (Royal Designer for Industry), the first woman to be awarded this distinction. Despite this, the opinion that she had a great influence on twentieth-century industrial design is hard to substantiate. Her work was seen by industrialists at the new design exhibitions such as the exhibition of British Industrial Art (known as the Dorland Hall exhibition) in 1933, where no doubt it was admired; but her only direct contact with industry was through R. Greg & Co.

Indirectly, however, Ethel Mairet's ideas percolated into industry through her students and associates from the workshop, Marianne Straub became a designer of great distinction, Joyce Griffiths designed samples for industry and taught at Hull College of Art, and Alastair Morton was the design director for his family's firm of Edinburgh Weavers (an offshoot of Morton Sundour Fabrics). Many others worked in art education and their students have subsequently gone into the textile industry most successfully although, at two removes, it is difficult fully to assess the effect.

CHAPTER 10
BEYOND THE WORKSHOP
1915-1952

After Ethel and Ananda Coomaraswamy parted in 1912, Ananda made over to his wife an allowance, first a lump sum and later income from investments in Ceylon. In 1939, for instance, this income amounted to about £50 a year which, together with her teaching fees and royalties from her books, gave her enough extra income to help her run the workshop. Not that she was ever well off; in order to finance her travels, she borrowed money from her sister Maud and on one occasion even sold her grand piano. The necessity to earn her own (and also her husband Philip's) living was, since 1913, a driving force behind her work, a force which continued throughout her lifetime. This partly accounts for her dislike of amateurs and her slight wariness of the Guild of Weavers, Spinners and Dyers, founded in Ditchling in 1931.

From the early days of the weaving studio at Shottery, Ethel Mairet tackled the publicising and selling of her work herself. An early public exhibition (the exact date is not known) was advertised at "The Weaving Room, The Thatched House", where her weavings were shown in the company of work by Wentworth Huyshe and William Mark, artists of the Campden connection, and the studio potter William Fishley Holland. Her first London showing was in 1915, at the Englishwoman Exhibition in the Central Hall, Westminster, and in 1916 she exhibited with the Arts and Crafts Exhibition Society.

After the First World War, a rash of arts and crafts exhibitions spread throughout the calendar, continuing for the next twenty years or so, although the generic term bore little resemblance to their spiritual forebear, the Arts and Crafts Movement. These events had little in common with the professional exhibitions we know today, but were arranged as largely non-selective, genteel trade fairs with the craftsmen and artists in attendance, ready to sell their wares or to take orders. As well as setting standards of price for their work, these exhibitions acted as a platform for ideas and an opportunity for cross-fertilization between the often remotely based craftsmen. A study of the exhibition catalogues reveals a wealth of activity in weaving, spinning and dyeing; Ethel Mairet's workshop was rivalled by at least half a dozen other establishments, many run by her former apprentices.

Ethel Mairet would arrive at such occasions with her weavings rolled up and packed in a couple of hold-alls. Preparation went almost unnoticed in the workshop and there was never any panic to finish things in time for an exhibition. The display was rudimentary: items were pinned to walls and strewn across tables, the primary object being to sell. A few of the more trusted girls from the workshop manned the stands at the London exhibitions, but Ethel Mairet always went herself to the Red Rose Guild Exhibition held each autumn in Manchester until, with the outbreak of war in 1939, craftsmen stopped attending in person.

In addition to these collaborative ventures, Ethel Mairet had connections with several small crafts shops and galleries. In London the Three Shields, 8 Holland Street, off Kensington High Street, run by Dorothy Hutton, and the Little Gallery in Ellis Street, off Sloane Street, run by Muriel Rose, were her two principal selling outlets. From its inception in 1922, the Three Shields stocked the work of many now-famous figures of the crafts revival, among them Bernard Leach, Michael Cardew and Ethel Mairet, and the owner was herself a practising calligrapher who undertook royal commissions. Dorothy Hutton let a room to Ethel Mairet for a period of ten days every six months or so, at a charge of £15; she recalls that the madder red fabrics were the most popular, and that "it was always a very happy arrangement".[1] It lasted until 1932 or 1933, but Ethel Mairet continued to deal with the Three Shields in a very limited way until 1945 when the gallery changed hands.

Working at the Three Shields between about 1922 and 1927 was a young woman called Muriel Rose; she quickly realised that she too could run a gallery and with a partner Peggy Turnbull she set out to find premises. The Little Gallery, formerly a laundry receiving shop, was very plain and white inside, with windows front and back and a skylight; in later years it expanded sideways and into a basement. The opening exhibition in 1928 showed the pottery of Katharine Pleydell-Bouverie and Norah Braden; the work of many other craftsmen was stocked, the chief textile exhibitors

The Red Rose Guild Exhibition at Houldsworth Hall, Manchester in 1931. Both photographs courtesy of the Red Rose Guild

throughout being the block printers Phyllis Barron and Dorothy Larcher. At the outset, most of the weavings exhibited were by Mary Kemp but, after the closure of the New Handworkers' Gallery and the ending of her regular arrangement with the Three Shields, Ethel Mairet held her London exhibitions at the Little Gallery. There were special exhibitions of Ethel Mairet's work in 1934, 1937 and 1938 but lengths were always held as part of the regular stock. During her exhibitions Ethel Mairet was very much in charge. She had her own yellow cards printed and on the first day she would arrive in a taxi from Victoria Station with the weavings, which she rapidly hung on the walls. Nothing was ever discussed in advance with the gallery proprietors and Ethel Mairet arranged to meet her clients personally.

Despite their early success in gaining commissions for the fabric printers Barron and Larcher, the owners of the Little Gallery never sold large quantities of Ethel Mairet's furnishings. Muriel Rose thought this was probably because the fabric was not in sufficiently long lengths for curtains, and yet was not hardwearing enough to be made into loose covers. The garments, made up at Ditchling, had little or no regard for fashion and, although Gospels produced more modernist cloth from about 1933, the styles of the clothes did not make the same advance until about 1940.

The Little Gallery closed with a grand sale on the outbreak of war in 1939. Roughly simultaneous with its opening, however, had been the advent of the New Handworkers' Gallery at 14 Percy Street, near Tottenham Court Road; it was run by Philip Mairet but had most likely been the brainchild of Ethel Mairet. The location, although close to the fashionable Heal's, was not good and the interior was worse; furthermore the gallery had to be reached by a steep flight of stairs and was not obviously visible from the street. Margery Kendon, at that time an apprentice at Gospels, has described it as "a back room on the first floor, too small to show the work to advantage, but it was a start, a pied-à-terre in London".[2] The gallery served as a base for Philip Mairet who wrote his articles for *The New Age* there and made frequent visits to Mitrinovic, to whom he was still philosophically attached. He was also planning a series of pamphlets on the crafts and the first three were published between 1928 and 1930, printed on hand-made paper by Douglas Pepler at the Ditchling Press. The titles were *The Idea behind Craftsmanship* by Philippe Mairet (using the French form of his Christian name), *Instead of a Catalogue (The Apologia of a Furniture Maker)* by A. Romney Green, *A Potter's Outlook* by Bernard Leach and *Art and Manufacture* by Eric Gill. *The Eurythmics of Jacques Dalcroze* by Valerie Cooper was published shortly before the gallery closed.

A lengthy correspondence for the New Handworkers' Gallery survives,

The New Handworkers
Gallery 6 Fitzroy Square W I

E. Mairet & G. Norsworthy

Fitzroy 1464

A display from the New Handworkers' Gallery and (above) the card printed in 1930 when the gallery moved premises, with Gwendoline Norsworthy as joint manager

indicating that talks were also organised on subjects akin to those covered by the pamphlets and that the scope of the stock was indeed wide. Among the regular exhibitors were "all the usual crowd" – Mairet, Barron and Larcher, Cardew, Leach, Romney Green – but the gallery also showed the less widely celebrated: weavers such as KilBride, Jewson, Doncaster, the metalsmiths Thornton and Downer, and the silversmith and wood craftsman Fred Partridge. More surprising was the inclusion of leatherwork, baskets, painted hats and lampshades and a quantity of Yugoslavian items gleaned originally from the Mairets' trip in 1927 and re-ordered the following year. The letters also reveal that Gordon Russell Workshops ordered cotton bed-spreads in 1930 in a quantity which must have caused pandemonium at Gospels.

In November 1930, as we have already seen, the New Handworkers' Gallery moved to 6 Fitzroy Square under the joint names of Ethel Mairet and Gwendoline Norsworthy. But this was followed almost immediately by the break between Ethel and Philip Mairet and the gallery was forced to close.

Since the early twenties Ethel Mairet had run an unofficial "shop" at Gospels on Saturdays and Sundays. It consisted of a long table of textiles in the weaving room, all along the window side, with rugs and garments hung up on the walls. Apart from the products of the workshop, she sold earthen-ware country pottery from her native North Devon and studio pottery by Cardew and Leach; there were wooden buttons and buckles by Fred Partridge, copies of the dyebook and, in the thirties, Yugoslavian belts and socks. The Gospels stock always included plenty of small items: tam-o'-shanters or berets made from offcuts of woven cloth, scarves (frequently woven by Ethel Mairet herself) and, after 1940, gloves (usually knitted by her from remnants of woollen yarn). People came specially to Ditchling to buy or order goods and increasingly, with the publication of Ethel Mairet's second book *Hand-Weaving To-day* in 1939, to visit the workshop.

With the demise of the New Handworkers Gallery, the Three Shields became Ethel Mairet's London base, where once a week she met clients. In 1933 she decided to terminate this arrangement and shortly afterwards she opened her own shop in Brighton. 68a East Street was a small shop owned by the artist and writer Tom Heron and his firm Cresta; it had previously been leased to Sybil Rigby, a hand-weaver trained at Gospels, who had run it for about ten years as a studio and shop. Ethel Mairet inherited from her an assistant, Thora Orchard, who managed the business under her direction. Thora Orchard has described the shop's appearance during the 1930s: "What always looked awfully nice in the shop were the layers of material stacked

Three of the pamphlets produced at the New Handworkers' Gallery, 1928–30

on the open shelves. The colours looked lovely because they were all either natural, white and black etc., or vegetable dyes. And the same remark applied to anything that was displayed in the window because the textures and colours were very attractive."[3]

During the War, the shop did unexpectedly well on the rationing system. Thora Orchard was called up to work on the land and Scilla Light took over the business, running it with an even freer hand; Ethel Mairet never criticised or made suggestions but made weekly visits "as a friend".

The business was run as a dress shop rather than a craft shop, the only other merchandise being Fred Partridge's buttons in carved, inlaid and poker-worked woods, and Yugoslavian slipper-socks and gloves. The two saleswomen, although they claimed not to have influenced the weaving, made improvements to the design of the clothes. The djibbahs and jerkins persisted until the early 1940s, but customers were also encouraged to select other simple shapes suitable for cutting from the loosely woven fabric. Thora Orchard commented, "I always discussed the style with the customers and we decided it together. One always had a *Vogue* handy anyway, to give an idea."[4]

The brightly coloured silk and cotton plaids designed by Ethel Mairet from 1938 were made up into jackets which sold very well; on her return from the shop she would infuriate the few overworked weavers with the phrase, "Mrs Light is clamouring." Ethel Mairet had created a very successful cloth and, as Scilla Light explains, even a new garment:

The jackets were really like a shirt top. Actually, I consider she really invented the shirtwaister – the little collar, the buttons down the front, the loose sleeves into a cuff, patch pockets – and you could wear this over a skirt or under a skirt. And of course she loved dirndls, Nellie Pullen [a Brighton dressmaker working for Ethel Mairet] surpassed herself at making these. Another thing was the table mats in raffia and cellophane; sometimes there was also a very fine thread with a thick knobbly look, that was very interesting. There was no material on the market that she wasn't prepared to use.[5]

The shirt-waister idea was also made up to order as a dress by Nellie Pullen, whom Ethel Mairet had recently discovered working near the art school in Brighton. Previously much of the dressmaking had been done by Miss Gull, by then restricted to making berets but who had in her time spun, cooked and cleaned at Gospels. A Mrs Browett is also recorded as having worked as a dressmaker (shared with Valentine KilBride) in 1940, and in the thirties several of the foreign girls had made up the clothes. For tailored woollen jackets, however, customers at the East Street shop in Brighton were advised to take the fabric round the corner to Mr Ayliffe, a gentleman's tailor and cutter. He would make very stylish fully lined and detailed jackets which bore no resemblance to the clothes of a decade earlier associated with Ethel Mairet. To obtain such lengths of wool Scilla Light is said to have raided Gospels and taken every bit of fabric she could. Another innovation was knitted jerseys in thick, soft Maltese cotton, which Mrs Light described as "very chic, sometimes they were smart enough for evening wear"[6]; unfortunately none have survived.

Scilla Light continued to run the Brighton shop until about 1945; she clearly made it in an artistic success and, quite possibly, a financial success also. For the remainder of the decade various people took turns in the shop's management, and by this time 68a East Street was the single regular selling outlet for Gospel's weaving. The shop continued until about 1951, when the lease expired.

The exhibitions in which Ethel Mairet took part during the forties reflected her increased status as a leader in hand-woven textiles and a Royal Designer for Industry. These were thematic exhibitions rather than selling outlets, organised in 1940, 1941 and 1942 by the British Council, in 1945 by the Association of Industrial Artists (AIA), and in 1943 and 1945 by the Council for the Encouragement of Music and the Arts (CEMA). Meanwhile she did not neglect the selling ventures: the Arts and Crafts Exhibition Society, the Red Rose Guild and the Scottish Society of Women Artists, and she also had work in other galleries round the country. Gauze (leno) curtains were shown at the National Gallery in CEMA's "Design at Home" exhibition of 1945, and neither the newly developed cellophane and jute wallcoverings nor the looped jute and parachute cord rugs would have been out of place. New fabrics exploiting Greg's fancy cotton yarns were shown in the British Council's exhibition at the Metropolitan Museum of Art in New York in 1942. Few of these textiles were woven by Ethel Mairet herself but were the products of the transient body of weavers, students and teachers who found at Gospels a sympathetic atmosphere in which to work.

Partly due to the British Council's exhibitions, the workshop was by now gaining exposure outside Britain; Ethel Mairet had first shown her work at Copenhagen in October 1932, where she delivered a lecture ambitiously entitled "The Cultural Importance of Hand-Loom Weaving". When she first started weaving, she had been consulted by Gandhi, who advocated the revival of the peasant economy in India; Gandhi was aware of the Coomaraswamys' work on the arts and crafts of Ceylon and also found much to sympathise with in A. K. Coomaraswamy's nationalist writings. On a visit to London he therefore met Ethel Mairet and they discussed the organisation of spinning and weaving in Indian villages; at that time Ethel Mairet was studying vegetable dyeing and she advocated its use in place of imported aniline dyes.

Closer to home her advice was also sought by the Royal Industries Bureau who, endeavouring to inject new life into the Welsh woollen industry, appointed Marianne Straub as designer on her recommendation. The Rural Industries Bureau regularly directed enquiries on hand-weaving to Ethel Mairet and her relationship with its Director, F. R. I. Brooke, was a fruitful one. The contribution she made, on this and other occasions, was largely through words which, by the late thirties, had become her chief tool for projecting her ideas.

CHAPTER 11
TEACHING AND
WRITING
1939-1952

Between 1939 and 1949 Ethel Mairet published three books with Faber and Faber. In 1938 she began *Hand-Weaving To-day*, her most successful book, greeted with wide acclaim by the Press. It came 22 years after her first book, *A Book on Vegetable Dyes* (1916), which had been more in the nature of a manual; the dyebook subsequently went into nine editions, from 1916 to 1946.

The introduction to *Hand-Weaving To-day*, subtitled "Traditions and Changes", explains her view of weaving:

It has more responsibility to the machine than any other craft. It is harder to become a well-trained weaver than a well-trained metal or leather worker or a printer. There are more things to be learnt and a more varied technique to be acquired. The essence of hand-weaving is in its continual creativeness and flexibility (this is also its danger), based strictly on traditional knowledge. It is dependent on architecture and clothing; it must work in close collaboration with both. It cannot ever be an art, by itself (as a beautifully printed book can be, or a fine piece of metal work), for always it must be part of a building (curtains, rugs, hangings, etc.) or associated with the necessities of life (clothes, tablecloths, towels).[1]

In her view the Arts and Crafts Movement, following Morris's influence, had isolated the individual craftsman and separated him from industrial development, but at the same time it had also saved him from extinction. She continues by presenting the dilemma, "A new orientation of the crafts must be found, a new idea of where they stand in relation to machinery."[2] But she does not say what expression this should take. She quotes Nikolaus Pevsner and Herbert Read, who in books published in the thirties had both tackled the rôle of the industrial designer, stressing the need for new aesthetic standards for mechanical production.

After a subjective account of contemporary hand-weaving in Europe, the book goes on to describe the materials obtainable or in use at the time, and gives a short history and description of their characteristics. Synthetic materials are given a prominent place, with the proviso that they are only to be used by artists with vision. A short section of the book is devoted to the teaching of textile crafts, and here she expresses regret that England has no proper training schools like those in other European countries.

In her next two books, Ethel Mairet enlarged on this theme and made practical suggestions for teachers in schools to work with. *Hand-Weaving and Education* (1942) covers little new ground, but *Hand-Weaving Notes for Teachers* (1949) shows an even greater enthusiasm for new materials and techniques. It names the areas of possible development as "(1) the use of synthetic yarns, (2) a new expression of machine embroidery, (3) the right understanding of the printing of textiles, and (4) a development of imaginative knitting".[3] In *Notes for Teachers* she also shows a growing acceptance of chemical colours, although she still maintained they were more difficult to use successfully.

Certain writers held a great fascination for her. In her library were books by Walt Whitman, popular in Campden days, Morris, Ruskin, Patrick Geddes and Lewis Mumford, whose *Technics and Civilization* she had specially bound into three volumes for travelling; the book grapples with man's development in an industrial age, stressing the needs of the individual in modern society. She was also greatly impressed by the writings of the architect Frank Lloyd Wright on modern building and planning, and she attended his lectures in London; she became an enthusiast for the new architecture.

The newly formed Guild of Weavers, Spinners and Dyers organised a series of summer schools in the mid 1930s, in which Ethel Mairet was involved. She realised that increasingly more people wanted short-term instruction and in the late 1930s she began a series of courses for teachers. The courses brought a new kind of person to Gospels, different from those who had attended the dye weeks since the mid twenties. These teachers and student-teachers came with notebooks and sketchbooks at the ready, demanding information; Ethel Mairet was convinced that what they really needed was enlightenment.

In her recently resumed correspondence with A. K. Coomaraswamy, she described the visit made in April 1941 by five students from Birmingham College of Art: "It was the first time that officially the Art School horrors had recognised the workshop – and it was a fine beginning."[4]

The courses were not really arranged and Ethel Mairet gave hardly any instruction; students had to learn by observation, including the rather "individual" method employed for putting on a warp. Barbara Sawyer attended the course in 1941: "Because we wove on the warps she had planned and set up, and used weft from her great and exciting store of yarns, and were surrounded on all sides by her own weaving, weaving she had collected, the samples we wove were very obviously characteristically 'Gospels'. Also we were pretty young – no-one over 22."[5]

An order book from Gospels, running from 1942 to 1944, shows that students and teachers came as individuals as well as in groups arranged by educational institutions; they were charged by the day for "weaving and house". This income, together with the sale of fabric, scarves, books and weaving materials, helped to support Ethel Mairet during the War. To make ends meet, she also sold eggs and vegetables to her pupils. At least 40 people passed through the workshop between 1938 and 1945; some of them had an effect on the weaving produced at Gospels, and many others went on to take Ethel Mairet's doctrines into education.

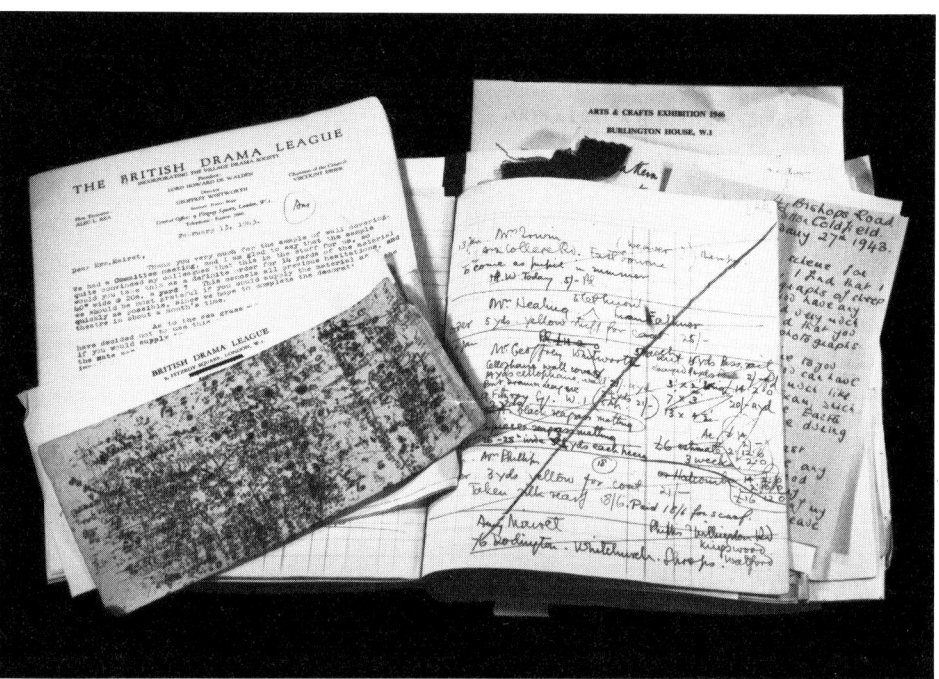

The Gospels order book, 1942–4

In 1939 Ethel Mairet was offered her only official teaching post, as part-time lecturer in weaving at Brighton School of Art (previously held by Valentine KilBride). The students, from the Department of Dress, studied weaving on Fridays and Saturdays. Their main subject was taught in the early 1940s by Miss Edith Solomon, who joined in on the weaving class and became a friend and client at Gospels.

The educational work started by the short courses for teachers was further expanded by Ethel Mairet's "textile portfolios", information packs intended for use in schools and colleges; these were distributed by post at a charge of 2s 6d per week. The portfolios contained a systematic and simplified study of weaving, spinning and dyeing. They also covered the identification of sheep breeds and fleeces, various man-made and natural fibres (spun and unspun) and examples of historical or modern foreign weaving. The latter were rarely seen outside museums and teaching of this kind was not yet widely introduced, even in books. Ethel Mairet's letters to Ananda Coomaraswamy explain her motives in planning the portfolios:

One of the things I am fighting hard for is decentralisation, which the War at the moment is making possible. Museums have done their work; it is now their job to decentralise, to spread out and keep moving. Their static period should be over, and people all over the country – or the world for that matter – should be able easily to see these beautiful things that are buried in musuem. I have been working at this idea for years. I expect I told you of one point I had reached: Lancashire Education Committee people, two or three years ago, asked me to make a collection of modern and traditional weaving that could travel round the various elementary schools – things that the children and teacher, could handle and that would be an inspiration to their taste and work. It was a great success. Essex did the same – Cambridgeshire was going to have one, but the War stopped it. So now I am making a library of textiles which the training colleges and schools can hire (for not more than a week or two, to prevent static conditions and copying). It is an exceedingly fascinating job, for me, and schools are finding it most useful – which is what I want.[6]

This letter was written in January 1941 when she had prepared seventeen portfolios (there were many duplicates of each); in April of the same year she wrote to Ananda again, mentioning the pamphlets which accompanied them:

At the moment I am writing a series of short pamphlets on weaving for teachers. It's the kind of thing that's badly wanted. Not teaching them *how* to weave – that can only be learnt in a workshop – but the background and foundations of weaving, as it must be again. It has been so basely treated and forgotten, what with the machine development and the using of the machine solely for money-making, and the forgetting how the roots of weaving lie so deeply in all of us. I will send you a copy of the first one. Badly written of course as I am not a student of writing – but only a talker. But I want to get over the few ideas I have before it is too late. One may be bombed at any time![7]

From the late thirties there were more short-course students at Gospels than apprentices. This was due partly to the increasing number of crafts courses in art schools and colleges, and also to conditions during the War, including lack of access to the south coast. The War nipped many schemes in the bud; the weaving school for which Ethel Mairet had published a prospectus in 1939–40 had to be abandoned. The production of cloth, especially the more experimental weaves in wool and silk, was severely curtailed by the shortage of raw materials and labour. Almost all the regular workgirls were called to more urgent duties for the War effort, leaving only Marjorie Denman and a workgirl called Nellie in the workshop by September, 1941.

The falling-off of momentum was a setback from which Ethel Mairet's work was never fully to recover; from then on her personal motivation was concentrated on her writing, but she repeatedly tried to re-invigorate the workshop by encouraging various trained weavers and designers to work temporarily at Gospels. During the winter of 1939 Leonora Maas from the Rural Industries Bureau's Welsh scheme came to Gospels and perfected the leno (gauze) technique for furnishings and shawls. She was particularly interested in technical matters and, with Ethel Mairet's approval (but not her interest), set up a cloth construction class in the attic for Kitty Akehurst and the other workgirls. She quite possibly taught them how to make the leno dupes for the weaving of her gauze designs, continued during the early forties. This episode stands out as one of the few technical advances in weaving made at Gospels, for although in 1944 Ethel Mairet had purchased a draw-loom she never knew how to use it, nor did she attempt to learn.

Cotton was the dominant fibre in the workshop from the end of the 1930s but a number of thicker, coarser fibres were also experimented with, partly as a result of Ethel Mairet's travels in Europe in 1938 and also out of necessity when wool and silk became unobtainable during the War. One of the first materials to change the scale of the weaving produced at Gospels was rag strip, inspired by the rag rugs purchased earlier in Berlin and woven in many experimental samples by Kate Crofton, who attended short courses in 1936 and 1938. On the courses double weave was also still in evidence, on warps originally planned by Marianne Straub.

From 1942, when she first attended a short course at Easter, a talented

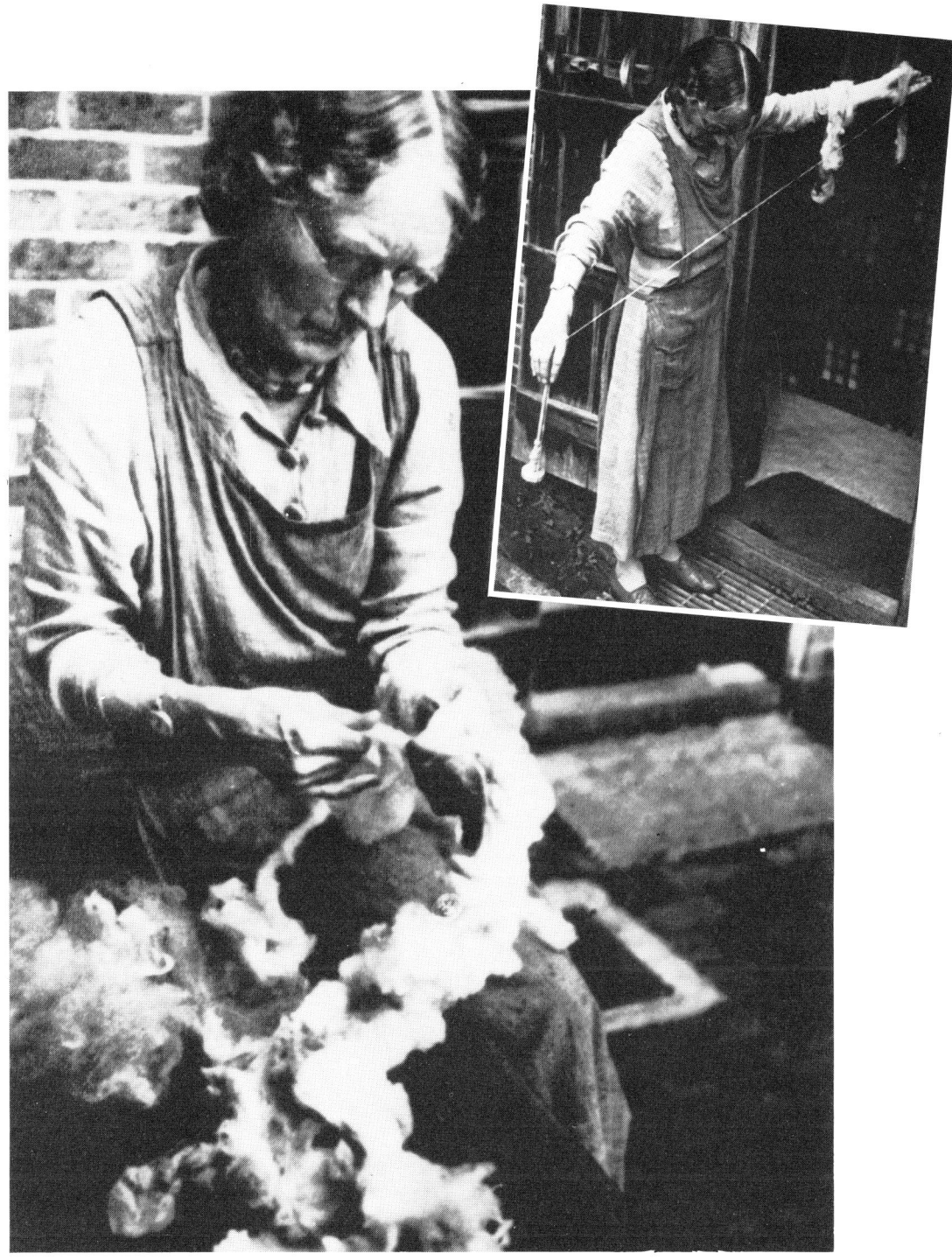

Ethel Mairet demonstrating the preparation of fleece and (inset) spindle spinning, 1945

young weaver named Barbara Sawyer was a regular vacation visitor to Gospels. She was interested in unusual fibres such as raffia and cellophane, and she made rugs incorporating loops, tufts or knots of jute inlaid in the weft. Her interest was shared by Ethel Mairet who tirelessly sought out different weavable fibres. Barbara Sawyer also wove table mats out of unspun jute, raffia or cellophane on a spaced cotton warp. A larger version of the same themes was woven, probably by Ethel Mairet, on a hemp warp and sold as a wallhanging or wall fabric to cover an entire wall surface.

A contemporary of Barbara Sawyer's at Gospels was Esmé Davis, who originally attended the workshop for half a day a week – "immersed in the colours and textures there"[8] – whilst teaching at Worthing School of Art, until in 1944 she became Ethel Mairet's assistant for six months. She took a particular interest in spindle spinning and made a series of drawings from the collection of historic and foreign spindles at Gospels. She also assembled a number of sample cards of hand-plied, wheel- and machine-spun yarns, which give an accurate picture of the fibres used in the workshop in 1943: jute, hemp, ramie (from Edinburgh Weavers), flax, rayon mixtures and staple fibres (from Courtaulds).

During the same period a very fine spinner, Barbara Hoather, spent vacations at Gospels; she was in charge of crafts at Bishop Otter Teacher Training College in Chichester and later went on to teach at Bromley School of Art. She was greatly admired by Ethel Mairet and also by her students, several of whom she encouraged to spend time at Gospels. Joy Sinden, one of these students, has related that, although she died tragically young, Barbara Hoather influenced innumerable students and that "most, if not all, her teaching was based on Mrs Mairet's ideas. . . . Temperamentally she was very much like Mrs Mairet and, like her, an excellent teacher."[9]

In winter 1944 the weaver-designers Marianne Straub and Alastair Morton both stayed at Gospels. Marianne Straub designed for her employers Helios in the mornings and worked for Ethel Mairet in the afternoons. Her work at the time was finer than before; she used several of Greg's plain and fancy cottons in pale colours on a spaced warp, or used methods of "reeding" to create light modern textiles for blouses or furnishing fabric. Her technical knowledge was equalled by Alastair Morton, described by Fiona MacCarthy as one of the "early design entrepreneurs".[10] His family's firm, Edinburgh Weavers, had successfully combined art and industry, and as early as 1927 his father, Sir James Morton, had said: "We have been provided by science with the most wonderful tools and materials but that is

Opposite: Ethel Mairet winding a bobbin, Gospels, c. 1945. By Courtesy of CoSIRA

not enough. We must add to them that alchemy which alone can make them into things of living beauty."[11] A frequent visitor to Ditchling, Alastair Morton came in search of that alchemy, and in return he probably brought with him some of the yarns produced by his firm, including a cotton chenille and a fibrous ramie (a yarn produced from a plant similar to the nettle).

During the last seven years of the Gospels workshop the principal designer-weavers were Hilary Bourne (1944–5), Dorothy Ablett (1950–51), Peter Collingwood (1950–51) and Mary Barker (1950–52), all of whom are still weaving today. Hilary Bourne and Dorothy Ablett (both trained weavers) were employed to experiment with new designs using existing yarns, in order to introduce some variation. After 1945 a Mrs Bennet was the only regular weaver recorded: she "threw the shuttle" for the production of lengths for the shop in Brighton. Dorothy Ablett parcelled up the textile portfolios, which still travelled widely. Of particular interest on the looms at this time was the reappearance of the woollen yarn sent from Morgan's in Wales; woven into a spotted double-cloth, it was made up into fashionable three-quarter length coats with raglan sleeves.

Contemporary with Dorothy Ablett, Peter Collingwood arrived as Ethel Mairet's last apprentice. Coming from a medical background and a short career in the Army, he found the environment unorthodox and the atmosphere strained. More than once he had differences with Ethel Mairet:

The strange thing for me was that to everybody else that went to her she was a sort of goddess. They had had a great build-up, they knew other weavers and every other weaver said "Oh, you must go to Ethel Mairet," and I knew nobody else so that when I went to her I thought that everything she did was *normal*. This was part of the friction between us two: the fact that I didn't look up to her; I just thought that what she did was what every weaver did.

I learnt to weave quite fast and I can remember weaving some tablemats in black cellophane weft, quite narrow, perhaps a quarter of an inch wide, and quite advanced for that time. I had imbibed this idea that one should always experiment; so I thought I would be clever and I would get a black cotton yarn and on the spinning wheel I would wind the cellophane round the cotton yarn, then I would be able to wind it on a bobbin and throw it across more easily. And she found me doing it and said "What on earth are you doing? I told you to weave black cellophane mats." I said that I thought I was developing something new, and she said "Go and do the mats, you can't have any lunch till they are done!" She *was* quite fierce.[12]

Despite this, Collingwood learnt to weave and spin and went on to have what Ethel Mairet termed "a critical workshop".[13] He names her, with Alastair Morton and Barbara Sawyer, in whose workshops he also studied, as the three best teachers a hand-weaver could have gone to.

By the end of the decade Ethel Mairet was the only remaining member of the old group left in Ditchling. Fred and Maud had died in 1946 and 1948 respectively, and Edward Johnston and Eric Gill had died a few years earlier. One of Ethel Mairet's last letters to Ananda, written in 1945, was sadly and uncharacteristically self-reproachful:

For a time our lives developed very much on the same lines then, quite rightly, you went on one way and I on another. But I feel very certain that if we had not had those years together we should neither of us have been such distinguished people. And if we had stuck together we should probably have hurt each other very badly. Just as PAM and I agreed to stick to each other for ten years and then we let the time go by, which was a mistake. But you never deceived me and PAM did. That I find exceedingly difficult to understand, even now. I have come to the conclusion it is something in myself that is wrong. I am good up to a certain point and then I just go off the deep end. I did with you; and I see now that I behaved abominably after a very lovely life with you. I could have been much nicer and more reasonable – more womanly perhaps and more forgiving and understanding. That is all past. I don't regret any part of my life. It is part of my make-up. And we both have had a better life because of it. I love work and I love risk. Ever since I left you I have crept along, always in debt, always on the edge of disaster but never quite – always overdrawn, always borrowing. But it has been worth while.[14]

Ananda's reply was sympathetic and philosophic. He then describes his own plans:

In a few years more we plan to go home to India (northern) permanently, when I will in a certain way retire, rather than dying in harness: that is, I want to contact and realise more immediately the actuality of the things of which my present knowledge is more "intellectual" than direct.[15]

But in 1947 Ananda Coomaraswamy died and Ethel Mairet destroyed all his letters, dating back to his travels in India in 1910. Her own health was failing.

Even in the 1950s, when she was nearly 80, Ethel Mairet still gave short demonstrations and had teachers or weavers staying at the house for weekends. Her neighbour Mary Hill describes her at this time: "she had a wonderful trust in life and people; alone and unafraid towards the end of her life . . . her family gone, with few visitors, her only constant companions the three Siamese cats, difficulties in making ends meet, she still presented a challenge to the timid."

Mary Barker, a weaver with industrial design and teaching experience, was a frequent visitor; she originally came to the area to take up Ethel Mairet's former teaching post at Brighton School of Art. The two women had many things in common, as well as professional differences. In the evenings Ethel Mairet would talk about her plans for her next book (which she was writing when she died) and would ask Mary Barker questions about her training at Leeds University, to "check her facts, in a way".[16] Some of her ideas would inflame Ethel Mairet: her support of chemical dyes, used sensitively, or the use of a raddle, a simple device used to spread the warp. When the raddle appeared one day in the workshop, Ethel Mairet said, "Now, prove that this is useful." Fortunately Mary Barker was able to do so and to roll on one of Ethel Mairet's "creative warps" by herself. She often helped with technical adjustments to the looms and also wove small items (doing only what she could complete in a weekend) such as cushion covers, or openwork scarves and stoles with interesting borders. One foggy Sunday in 1952, when she was up in the gallery weaving scarves, Ethel Mairet called her down to help tie up a loom and complained from underneath: "I must be getting old, it's making me giddy down here."[17] The loom was tied up, Mary Barker finished her scarves and left early, promising to return in two weeks' time. But on 18 November 1952 Ethel Mairet was found dead, with her Siamese cats beside her on the bed. After the funeral Mary Barker returned to the workshop: "I did go in to see what she had done. And I thought, 'It's not bad to have done something creative on your last day of life.' . . . There was about a yard of thick-and-thin wool mixture on the big loom."[18]

In July 1952, the year of her death, an International Conference and Exhibition of Pottery and Textiles had been held at Dartington Hall in Devon. Ethel Mairet sent her work to the exhibition, where it was shown next to Marianne Straub's, but she was not able to attend the conference. It was an important event for the crafts, held in a progressive school and centre for cultural activities, and it was run on a truly international scale. The exhibition subsequently moved to London and two years later a report was published, giving a full account. The chief papers on textiles were by Alec Hunter, Aagot Poort, A. E. Southern and Marianne Straub. The discussion topics centred on the craftsman in relation to scientific development, the craftsman's ideals and the integration of the crafts into society. The conference was attended by a large group of young artists and craftspeople from seventeen countries who wished to learn from each other's experience in order to improve their own work. It was the kind of exchange of ideas that Ethel Mairet might well have dreamt of when she founded the Gospels workshop over thirty years before.

BIBLIOGRAPHY

Albers, Anni, *On Designing*, Wesleyan University Press (Middletown, Connecticut, 1962)

Albers, Anni, *On Weaving*, Wesleyan University Press (Middletown, Connecticut, 1965)

Anscombe, Isabelle, and Gere, Charlotte, *Arts and Crafts in Britain and America*, Academy Editions (London, 1978)

Ashbee, C. R., *Craftsmanship in Competitive Industry*, Essex House Press (Broad Campden, 1908)

Ashbee, C. R., *Modern English Silverwork*, Essex House Press (Broad Campden, 1909)

Ashbee, C. R., *Should We Stop Teaching Art?*, Batsford (London, 1912)

Ashbee, C. R., *Peckover: the Abbotscourt Papers*, Astolat Press (London, 1932)

Aslin, Elizabeth, *The Aesthetic Movement*, Ferndale Editions (London, 1981)

Baines, Patricia, *Spinning Wheels, Spinners and Spinning*, Batsford (London, 1977)

Briggs, Asa (ed.), *William Morris: Selected Writings and Designs*, Penguin (London, 1962)

Chetwynd, Hilary, *Simple Weaving*, Studio Vista (London, 1969)

Coomaraswamy, Ananda K., *Mediaeval Sinhalese Art*, Essex House Press (Broad Campden, 1908)

Coomaraswamy, Ananda K., *Indian Drawings*, vol. I, Essex House Press (Broad Campden, 1910)

Coomaraswamy, Ananda K., *Indian Drawings*, vol. II, India Society (London, 1912)

Coomaraswamy, Ananda K., *Art and Swadeshi*, Ganesh and Co. (Madras, 1911)

Cox, Peter (ed.), *Dartington Hall International Conference on Pottery and Textiles* (Dartington, Devon, 1954)

Emery, Irene, *The Primary Structures of Fabrics*, The Textile Museum (Washington, D.C., 1966)

Fitzrandolph, Helen E., and Doriel Hay, M., *Rural Industries in England and Wales*, Agricultural Economics Research Institute, Clarendon Press (Oxford, 1927)

Forbes, Colin (ed.), with introductory essay by Alan Crawford, *Robert Welch: Design in a Cotswold Workshop*, Lund Humphries (London, 1973)

Garner, Philippe (ed.), *Phaidon Encyclopedia of Decorative Arts 1890–1940*, Phaidon (London, 1978)

Glynn, Sean, and Oxborrow, John, *Interwar Britain: a social and economic history*, George Allen & Unwin (London, 1976)

Hooper, Luther, *Hand-Loom Weaving*, John Hogg (London, 1910)

Howard, Constance, *Twentieth-Century Embroidery in Great Britain to 1939*, Batsford (London, 1981)

Hunt, Antony, *Textile Design*, Studio Publications (London, 1937)

Johnston, Priscilla, *Edward Johnston*, Faber and Faber (London, 1959)

Leach, Bernard, *Hamada, potter*, Kodansha International (Tokyo, 1975)

Lipsey, Roger, *Coomaraswamy*, vol. III, *His Life and Work*, Bollingen Series 89, Princeton University Press (1977)

London County Council, *Teaching of Art and Artistic Crafts in London* (London, 1923)

MacCarthy, Fiona, *The Simple Life*, Lund Humphries (London, 1981)

MacCarthy, Fiona, *British Design since 1880*, Lund Humphries (London, 1982)

Mairet, Ethel, *A Book on Vegetable Dyes*, Hampshire House Press (London, 1916)

Mairet, Ethel, *Hand-Weaving To-day: Traditions and Changes*, Faber and Faber (London, 1939)

Mairet, Ethel, *Hand-Weaving and Education*, Faber and Faber (London, 1942)

Mairet, Ethel, *Hand-Weaving Notes for Teachers*, Faber and Faber (London, 1949)

Mairet, Philip, *A Memoir of A. R. Orage*, University Books Inc. (Secaucus, U.S.A., 1966)

Mairet, Philip (ed. C. H. Sisson), *Autobiographical and Other Papers*, Carcanet New Press (Manchester, 1981)

Morton, Jocelyn, *Three Generations in a Family Textile Firm*, Routledge & Kegan Paul (London, 1971)

Naylor, Gillian, *The Arts and Crafts Movement*, Studio Vista (London, 1971)

Pevsner, Nikolaus, *An Enquiry into Industrial Art in England*, Cambridge University Press (1937)

Ponting, K. G., *A Dictionary of Dyes and Dyeing*, Bell & Hyman (London, 1981)

Read, Herbert, *Art and Industry: the principles of industrial design*, Faber and Faber (London, 1934)

Rodier, Paul, *The Romance of French Weaving*, Tudor Publishing Co. (New York, 1931)

Sewell, Brocard, *St Dominic's Press, Ditchling: a checklist of publications 1916–1936*, Ditchling Press (1979)

Shewring, Walter (ed.), *Letters of Eric Gill*, Jonathan Cape (London, 1947)

Singam, S. Durai Raja, *Homage to A. K. Coomaraswamy* (privately published, Kuala Lumpur, 1947)

Singam, S. Durai Raja, *A Study of a World Figure* (privately published, Kuala Lumpur, 1973)

Singam, S. Durai Raja (ed.), *Ananda Coomaraswamy, Remembering and Remembering Again and Again* (privately published, Kuala Lumpur, 1974)

Singam, S. Durai Raja, *Ananda Coomaraswamy – The Bridge Builder, A Study of a Scholar Colossus* (privately published, Kuala Lumpur, 1977)

Singam, S. Durai Raja, *Who Is This Coomaraswamy?* (privately published, Kuala Lumpur, 1980)

Straub, Marianne, *Hand Weaving and Cloth Design*, Pelham Books (London, 1977)

Sutton, Ann, Collingwood, Peter and St Aubyn Hubbard, Geraldine, *The Craft of the Weaver*, BBC Publications (London, 1982)

Thompson, Paul, *The Work of William Morris*, William Heinemann (London, 1967)

Thompson, Paul, *The Voice of the Past: oral history*, Oxford University Press (Oxford, 1978)

Tomkinson, G. K., *A Select Bibliography of the Principal Modern Presses*, Curwen Press (London, 1928)

Vasina, Jan, *Oral Tradition: a study in historical methodology*, Routledge & Kegan Paul (London, 1965)

Waller, Irene, *Fine Art Weaving*, Batsford (London, 1979)

Yorke, Malcolm, *Eric Gill: man of flesh and spirit*, Constable (London, 1981)

Journals

Aglaia, Journal of the Healthy and Artistic Dress Union, 1890–96 (later became *The Dress Review*)

The Art Journal, 1890–1912

Crafts, no. 50, 1981

Crafts Quarterly, issue 1, 1981

Design and Industries Association Journal, 1927–32 (later became *Design for Today*, 1933–6)

Dryad Quarterly, 1931–45

International Textiles, 1944–6

Oral History, journal of the Oral History Society

Quarterly News of the Guild of Weavers, Spinners and Dyers, 1933–9 (later became *Weavers Journal*)

Rural Industries, 1925–37

The Studio

Exhibition Catalogues

Applied Arts and Handcrafts Exhibition (London, 1934)

Arts and Crafts Exhibition Society (London, 1916, 1926, 1928, 1931, 1933 and 1935)

C. R. Ashbee and the Guild of Handicraft (Cheltenham Art Gallery, 1981)

Phyllis Barron and Dorothy Larcher (Crafts Study Centre, Bath, 1978)

British Art in Industry (Royal Academy, London, 1935)

British Industrial Art (Dorland Hall, London, 1933)

British Institute of Industrial Art Exhibition (London, 1922)

Dartington International Exhibition of Pottery and Textiles (Dartington, 1952)

Design at Work: Royal Designers for Industry (Royal Academy, 1948)

Englishwoman Exhibition (London, 1915, 1918 and 1920)

Exposition International des Arts Decoratifs, Industriels et Modernes (Paris, 1925)

First Exhibition of the Guild of Weavers, Spinners and Dyers (Whitechapel Art Gallery, 1935)

Homespun to Highspeed: a century of British design 1880–1890 (Sheffield City Art Galleries, 1979)

Modern British Crafts (shown in U.S.A.; published by the British Council, London, 1941)

William Morris and Kelmscott (West Surrey College of Art and Design; published by the Design Council, London, 1981)

Alastair Morton and Edinburgh Weavers (Scottish National Gallery of Modern Art, 1978)

Weaving by Elizabeth Peacock (Crafts Study Centre, Bath, 1979)

Red Rose Guild Exhibitions (Manchester, 1920–33, 1938, 1947–52)

Thirties (Hayward Gallery, 1979)

Twentieth-Century Craftsmanship (Crafts Study Centre, Bath, 1972)

Victorian and Edwardian Decorative Arts (Victoria and Albert Museum, London, 1952)

A Choice of Design 1850–1980: fabrics by Warner and Sons Ltd (touring exhibition, 1981)

SOURCES OF QUOTATIONS

The Ashbee Journals (40 volumes) are housed in the Modern Literary Archive at the library of King's College, Cambridge, where they may be consulted by arrangement with the Modern Archivist.

The Ethel Mairet Papers, the source material for this book, are housed in the Crafts Study Centre at the Holburne of Menstrie Museum in Bath. The Papers consist of letters, notes, manuscripts, photographs, travel journals, order books and the like dating from Ethel Mairet's life, supplemented by correspondence and transcripts of taped interviews made in 1981–3 during the preparation of this book and the accompanying exhibition. The Papers may be examined by appointment with the Curator of the Centre.

Chapter 2   Arts and Crafts in Ceylon 1903–1906

1   Lipsey, Roger, *Coomaraswamy*, vol. III, *His Life and Work*, Bollingen Series 89, Princeton University Press (1977), p. 20

2   *Ceylon Observer*, 1905, quoted in Lipsey, op. cit., p. 20

3   Coomaraswamy, Ananda K., *Mediaeval Sinhalese Art*, Essex House Press (Broad Campden, 1908), p. 242

4   Coomaraswamy, Ethel, ''Old Sinhalese Embroidery'', *Ceylon National Review*, July 1906, p. 119

5   Ibid

6   Morris, May (ed.), *The Collected Works of William Morris*, vol. XXII, Longmans, Green & Co. (London, 1910–15), p. 77

7   Coomaraswamy, Ananda K. and Ethel, ''Kandyan Horn Combs'', *Spolia Zeylanica*, October 1905, pp. 151–4

8   Coomaraswamy, Ethel, ''Embroidery and Dress'', *The Dress Review*, October 1906, pp. 67–72

9   Coomaraswamy, Ethel, ''The Dress Movement in Germany'', *The Dress Review*, no. 4, vol. 1, April 1903, pp. 39–42

10   Coomaraswamy, Ethel, ''English Dress in the Colonies'', *The Dress Review*, no. 4, vol. 1, October 1905, pp. 241–2

11   Coomaraswamy, Ethel, ''The Education of Girls in Ceylon'', *Journal of the Ceylon University Association*, October 1906, pp. 210–12

12   Coomaraswamy, Ethel, ''Music in Ceylon'', *Ceylon National Review*, January 1907, pp. 297–301

13   Coomaraswamy, Ethel, ''The Education of Girls in Ceylon'', op. cit., p. 212

14   The Ashbee Journals, autograph letter: Ethel Coomaraswamy to C. R. Ashbee, 14 March 1909

15   The Ashbee Drawings (Campden Trust), plan of the Norman Chapel annotated by Ethel Coomaraswamy, January 1906

16   Lipsey, op. cit., p. 42

17   See *Teaching Art and Artistic Crafts in London*, a pamphlet produced by London County Council, 1923; weaving was taught at only two London art schools, Blackheath Art School and the Central School of Arts and Crafts.

18   Coomaraswamy, Ananda K., *Mediaeval Sinhalese Art*, op. cit., p. 234

19   Notes on the techniques of weaving and dyeing are recorded in both Ethel and Ananda Coomaraswamy's notebooks and journals from Ceylon, now in the Firestone Library, Princeton University

20   The Ashbee Journals, autograph letter: Janet Ashbee to C. R. Ashbee, 14 April 1917

Chapter 3   The Norman Chapel 1907–1910

1   "The Norman Chapel Buildings, Broad Campden, Glos", *The Builder*, vol. 93, August 1907, p. 223

2   Ashbee, C. R., "The Norman Chapel Buildings at Broad Campden", *The Studio*, vol. 41, 1907, pp. 289–96

3   Account written by Alan Crawford, November 1982

4   The Ashbee Journals, entry written by Janet Ashbee, 26 January 1908

5   Mairet, Philip, quoted in Singam, S. Durai Raja, *Ananda Coomaraswamy, Remembering and Remembering Again and Again* (privately published, Kuala Lumpur, 1974), p. 323

6   The Ashbee Journals, entry written by Janet Ashbee, 26 January 1908

7   The Ashbee Journals, autograph letter: Ethel Coomaraswamy to C. R. Ashbee, 15 December 1908

8   The Ashbee Journals, autograph letter: Ethel Coomaraswamy to C. R. Ashbee, 5 February 1909

9   Ashbee, C. R., *Craftsmanship in Competitive Industry*, Essex House Press (Broad Campden, 1908), p. 10

10   The Ashbee Journals, autograph letter: Ethel Coomaraswamy to C. R. Ashbee, 14 March 1909

11   Mairet, Philip (ed. C. H. Sisson), *Autobiographical and Other Papers*, Carcanet New Press (Manchester, 1981), p. 69

12   Victoria and Albert Museum, autograph letter: Alec Miller to Peter Floud, 21 November 1954 (by permission of Jane Wilgress)

Chapter 4   "The Real and the Ideal" 1910–1913

1   Ethel Mairet Papers, India Journal, 28 July 1910

2   Ibid, 10 August 1910

3   The Ashbee Journals, autograph letter: Ethel Coomaraswamy to C. R. Ashbee, 14 September 1910

4   The Ashbee Journals, autograph letter: Ethel Coomaraswamy to C. R. Ashbee, 8 October 1910

5   The Ashbee Journals, autograph letter: Ethel Coomaraswamy to C. R. Ashbee, 8 January 1911

6   Mairet, Philip (ed. C. H. Sisson), *Autobiographical and Other Papers*, Carcanet New Press (Manchester, 1981), p. 53

7   Letter from Iona Smyth Reed to Margot Coatts, 20 May 1982

8   The Ashbee Journals, autograph letter: Janet Ashbee to C. R. Ashbee, 22 February 1912

9   Mairet, op. cit., pp. 71–2

Chapter 5   "A Return to Reason" 1913–1917

1   Coomaraswamy, Ethel, "The Future of Dyeing", Old Bourne Press (London, 1915)

2   Thompson, Paul, *The Work of William Morris*, William Heinemann (London, 1967), p. 102

3   Mairet, Philip (ed. C. H. Sisson), *Autobiographical and Other Papers*, Carcanet New Press (Manchester, 1981), p. 87

4   Selver, Paul, quoted in Mairet, Philip, *A Memoir of A. R. Orage*, University Books (Secausus, U.S.A., 1966), Reintroduction

5   The Ashbee Journals, autograph letter: Janet Ashbee to C. R. Ashbee, 14 April 1917

6   The Ashbee Journals, autograph letter: Fred Partridge to Janet Ashbee, 22 April 1917

7   Ibid

Chapter 6   The Move to Ditchling 1917–1920

1   Coomaraswamy, Ethel, *A Book on Vegetable Dyes*, Hampshire House Workshops (Hammersmith, 1916), Introduction

2   Ibid

3   Ibid

4   Ibid, publisher's note

5   The Ashbee Journals, autograph letter: Philip Mairet to C. R. Ashbee, 3 February 1919

6   Mairet, Ethel and P.A., "An Essay on Crafts and Obedience" (Ditchling, 1918), pp. 2–3

7   Ibid, pp. 6–8

Chapter 7   The Workshop at Gospels 1920–1930

1   Interview with Joan Partridge, 19 January 1982

2   Interview with Petra Tegetmeier, 27 April 1982

3   Interview with Joanna and Cecilia Kilbride, 15 January 1982

4   Leach, Bernard, *Hamada, potter*, Kodansha International (Tokyo, 1975), p. 59

5   Letter from Janet Leach to Margot Coatts, 21 February 1983

6   Ethel Mairet Papers, autograph letter from Kitty Doncaster to Alice Hindson, 25 May 1948

7   Interview with Petra Tegetmeier, 27 April 1982

8   Walker, Lynne and Sanger, C., "The Inval Weavers", *Craft Quarterly*, issue 1 (1981)

9   Interview with Petra Tegetmeier, 27 April 1982

10   Questionnaire completed by Doris Jewson, November 1982

11   Interview with Margery Kendon, 13 January 1982

12   Interview with Petra Tegetmeier, 27 April 1982

13   Interview with Margery Kendon, 13 January 1982

14   The Ashbee Journals, November 1923

Chapter 8   European Travels 1927–1938

1   Interview with Margery Kendon, 13 January 1982

2   Ethel Mairet Papers, Yugoslavia Journal I, 15 May 1927

3   Ethel Mairet Papers, Yugoslavia Journal II, 8 May 1930

4   Ibid, 21 May 1930

5   Ibid, 24 May 1930

6   Ethel Mairet Papers, Scandinavia Journal II, 20 June 1933

7   Ibid, 28 June 1933

8   Letter from K. R. Drummond to Margot Coatts, 28 June 1982

9   Ethel Mairet Papers, Scandinavia Journal III, 29 June 1936

10   Ethel Mairet Papers, Germany and Switzerland Journal, June 1938, p. 7

11   Ibid, p. 13

12   Ibid, p. 15

13   Ethel Mairet Papers, Wales Journal, 26 June 1937

Chapter 9   Developments at Gospels 1933–1938

1   Mairet, Philip, *A Memoir of A. R. Orage*, University Books (Secausus, U.S.A., 1966), Introduction

2   Letter from Mary Hill to Margot Coatts, July 1982

3   Interview with Hilary Bourne and Marjorie Kenney, 15 January 1982

4   Ibid

5   Ibid

6   Ethel Mairet Papers, undated manuscript entitled "Weaving School Plan", 1933

7   Pevsner, Nikolaus, *An Enquiry into Industrial Art in England*, Cambridge University Press (Cambridge, 1937), p. 55

8   Interview with Hilary Bourne and Marjorie Kenney, 15 January 1982

9   Ibid

10   Interview with Marianne Straub, 16 May 1982

11   Ethel Mairet Papers, ''The Workshops of Ethel Mairet'', pamphlet produced by Ethel Mairet in the early 1930s

12   Interview with Joyce Griffiths, 14 January 1982

13   Ethel Mairet Papers, autograph letter from Ethel Mairet to Marianne Straub, 11 December 1938

14   Interview with Stopford Jacks, 7 May 1982

15   Account written by Stopford Jacks, July 1982

16   Hunt, Antony, *Textile Design*, Studio Publications (London, 1937), p. 64

17   Pevsner, Nikolaus, op. cit., p. 188

Chapter 10   Beyond the Workshop 1915–1952

1   Autograph letter from Dorothy Hutton to Margot Coatts, 29 April 1982

2   Interview with Margery Kendon, 13 January 1982

3   Interview with Thora Orchard, 22 June 1982

4   Ibid

5   Interview with Scilla Light, 18 August 1982

6   Ibid

Chapter 11   Teaching and Writing 1939–1952

1   Mairet, Ethel, *Hand-Weaving To-day*, Faber and Faber (London, 1939), Introduction

2   Ibid, p. 23

3   Mairet, Ethel, *Hand-Weaving Notes for Teachers*, Faber and Faber (London, 1949), p. 34

4   Coomaraswamy Family Papers, autograph letter from Ethel Mairet to Ananda Coomaraswamy, April 1941

5   Notes made by Barbara Sawyer following an interview, 24 March 1982

6   Coomaraswamy Family Papers, autograph letter from Ethel Mairet to Ananda Coomaraswamy, 28 January 1941

7   Coomaraswamy Family Papers, autograph letter from Ethel Mairet to Ananda Coomaraswamy, 29 April 1941

8   Autograph letter from Esmé Davis to Heather Child, 6 September 1981

9   Questionnaire completed by Joy Sinden, November 1982

10   MacCarthy, Fiona, *British Design since 1880*, Lund Humphries (London, 1982), p. 120

11   Morton, James, talk given at The Textile Institute, Manchester, privately published in *To Young Weavers* (Carlisle, 1927)

12   Interview with Peter Collingwood, 19 May 1982

13   Ethel Mairet Papers, autograph letter from Ethel Mairet to Peter Collingwood, 26 December 1951

14   Coomaraswamy Family Papers, autograph letter from Ethel Mairet to Ananda Coomaraswamy, 5 May 1945

15   Coomaraswamy Family Papers, typed letter from Ananda Coomaraswamy to Ethel Mairet, 1 June 1945

16   Interview with Mary Barker, 7 February 1982

17   Ibid

18   Ibid

INDEX

Page numbers in *italics* refer to the illustrations